How To...
PLAY R&B SOUL KEYBOARDS

By Henry Soleh Brewer

HAL•LEONARD®
7777 W. BLUEMOUND RD. P.O. BOX 13819 MILWAUKEE, WI 53213

ISBN 978-1-4950-9320-3

In Australia Contact:
Hal Leonard Australia Pty. Ltd.
4 Lentara Court
Cheltenham, Victoria, 3192 Australia
Email: ausadmin@halleonard.com.au

Visit Hal Leonard Online at
www.halleonard.com

CONTENTS

4   Introduction

7   Chapter 1: Rhythm, Feel, and the Groove

13   Chapter 2: The Blues

18   Chapter 3: Gospel and Soul Keyboard Voicings

25   Chapter 4: Technique, Independence, and the Left Hand

32   Chapter 5: Piano, Organ, Strings, and Horns

40   Chapter 6: Rhythm & Blues Playing Examples

49   Chapter 7: Soul Grooves

53   Chapter 8: Soul Ballads

58   Chapter 9: L.H. Chords with R.H. Strings

62   Chapter 10: L.H. Chords with R.H. Horns

66   Resource Materials

69   Four Decades of Funk

70   Acknowledgments

71   About the Author

INTRODUCTION

In this book, we will examine the genesis of R&B soul keyboard playing. Anyone seriously interested in this musical style should listen to it as much as possible, noting its various characteristics, both obvious and subtle. Pay careful attention to how the keyboard is used and the role it plays in each song, stylistically and practically. Center your study on recordings, various books and articles, autobiographies, and video footage of the R&B soul artists themselves. Over time, you will develop an authentic R&B soul keyboard sound built upon what has become an American musical tradition.

The R&B soul musical style found its roots in early gospel and blues music. It was a style created and personified by Africans enslaved in America. African-Americans derived this music from the scales and harmonies used in African vocal and drum songs. These songs were used in traditional dance and celebration rituals performed by various nations on the continent of Africa. The African-Americans continued this tradition in spite of the limitations of slavery: the unique musical style of R&B soul music can be heard in early spiritual songs and was also evident in the field hollers of the slaves.

The History of African-American Music

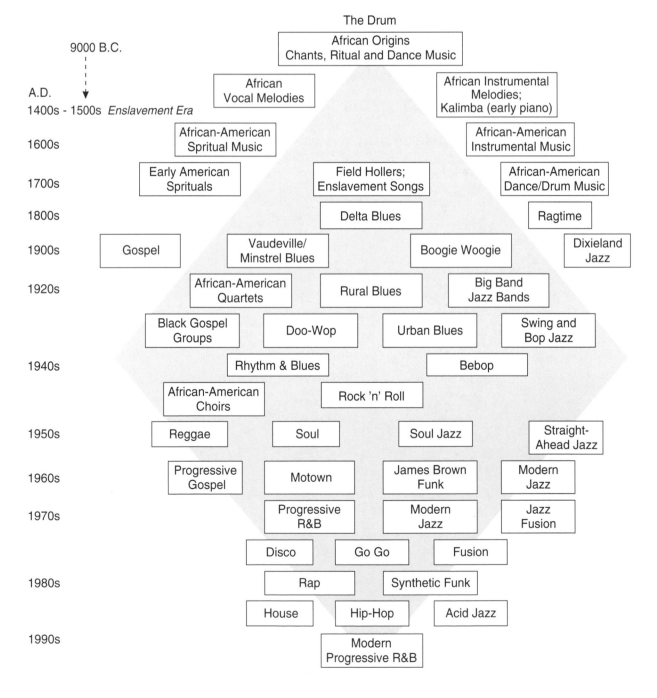

The Roots and Leaves of R&B

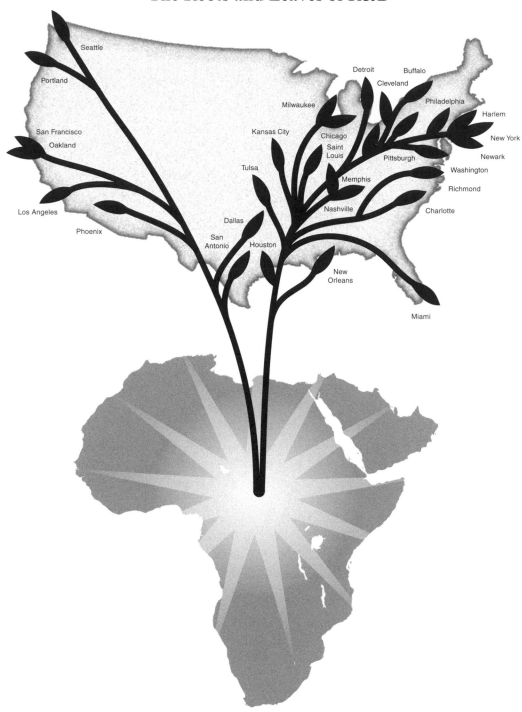

Early R&B soul music began as a result of African-Americans moving from the rural South into large cities "up North" to find factory work. This new way of life became evident in the way the music was interpreted. In the mid-1940s, R&B soul music found its origins. Much of the early 1950s R&B soul can be considered a cross of blues, gospel, doo wop, and rock 'n' roll. It wasn't until the early 1960s that R&B soul music fully evolved into what we know today. Just as we consider the guitar the instrument of rock and blues, we can consider the keyboard the instrument of R&B soul music, because it has dominated the genre from the 1970s to the present. In fact, from the piano and organ to modern synthesizers and samplers, the keyboard has revolutionized R&B soul music.

This book will clarify the differences between rhythm-and-blues and soul music. The disparities will be evident in the way certain examples are played. Many people cannot hear or understand the harmonic, rhythmic, melodic, and dynamic subtleties between these two styles. In the past, the media inferred that all black recordings were race records. Disc jockeys called the genre "the blues with rhythm" –

hence the imposed label "R&B." Soul music evolved from the styles of early R&B, doo wop, and black gospel music some time during the early 1960s, as the recording industry sought to simplify, categorize, and control the expansion and marketing of black music. This is how rhythm-and-blues and soul music became one name. We will also learn how blues and funk are related to R&B, just as gospel and doo wop are related to soul music.

Playing R&B soul keyboard was originally an extension of playing blues piano. To perform on R&B soul keyboards with the kind of flavor and attitude the style demands, we are required to understand blues piano playing to a certain extent; to that end, several common blues patterns and techniques will be presented.

We will study other practical concepts, as well as various playing techniques relative to R&B soul keyboards. In each chapter, there are examples for you to master and play along with the audio tracks. The topics we'll cover include: different left-hand (L.H.) and right-hand (R.H.) patterns, common R&B soul song forms, organ techniques, R&B comping for dance grooves and ballads, and effective voicings for R&B soul songs and patterns. The examples will encourage you to learn and grow into the R&B soul tradition and to play soulfully with confidence and authority.

A lot of people mistakenly believe R&B soul music is nothing more than a simple groove underneath elaborate vocal stylings. On the contrary, R&B soul can contain complex chord progressions, syncopated rhythms, or heavy African rhythms evident in other styles such as jazz, rock, Latin, Afro-Cuban, rap, hip-hop, reggae, and many others. Its influence can be heard around the world.

Lastly, to play R&B soul keyboards effectively, you must have experience to draw on. It is not the kind of music that allows you to learn one song and suddenly know all there is to know about it. This music is more than just playing notes; it is necessary to grasp the meaning of the music and its history. Once you learn that, then the music must be a part of you. R&B soul music requires an understanding of the culture this type of music evolved from. You have to get to know and respect the music and the people who created it.

Once the initial study has started and you find yourself beginning to see musical results from your efforts, it is logical to express it to others. All music is for healing and sharing. If you have listened to and taken pleasure in R&B soul music, you should then become compelled to emulate those artists whom you have enjoyed. It is from this imitation and deep understanding that you can share the experiences of others and play honestly with feeling. Your effort to perform R&B soul keyboards authentically will then genuinely heal and enrich anyone who listens to you.

Recording

Henry Brewer	keyboards, drum programming, guitar, bass, and arrangements
Sekou Olatunji	additional guitar
Freddie White	drums
Isis Nefetari Nubian	narration

Editor's Note: To access the audio tracks, use the unique code in the front of the book. You can listen online or download the tracks to your mobile device. The audio icons throughout the book correspond to the online tracks. Due to the number of recorded examples, some tracks may include more than one figure. All figures with a (P) after them are "playing examples" and have two parts: the figure played through once, and the figure played through without the keyboard parts, to allow you to practice with the recording.

Some keyboard patches do not have the same range as a standard piano. In certain instances, you may need to transpose parts down or up an octave, depending on your patch. Whenever this comes into question, match your range to the sound of the recorded track.

 Spoken Introduction

Track 1

CHAPTER 1

RHYTHM, FEEL, AND THE GROOVE

THE 1950s

Much of the character of early R&B music of the 1950s revolves around *rhythm*. The jump beats of that era provided a solid backbeat for what evolved into the Motown R&B soul sound. Early R&B piano players like Fats Domino used New-Orleans-inspired triplet patterns to provide light syncopation against a solid backbeat. Throughout the '50s, the stop, break, and hit patterns made famous by greats such as James Brown were common among piano players.

Ex. 1

Track 2

Other piano players, such as Little Richard, used straight-eighth-note patterns based on the shuffle patterns established by blues piano greats like Otis Span. Along with the aggressive R.H. eighth notes, R&B players were trilling, flailing, and glissing with reckless abandon for dynamic effects.

Ex. 2

Track 2
(cont'd)

THE 1960s

As the R&B soul sound developed into the 1960s, pianists began to use more black gospel rhythms. Piano techniques included pedaling the root-to-5th L.H. pattern and syncopated R.H. chord patterns. Piano parts also became more diverse, often including single-line and octave patterns. During the '60s, the arrangements grew to include more strings and guitars, so the piano's rhythm had to become stronger and a greater part of the rhythm section.

Ex. 3

Track 2
(cont'd)

The Organ

Many R&B soul keyboard players started to incorporate the organ into their playing; by the early-to-mid-1960s, it was common to play either piano or organ. When an organist was used, he or she normally played sustained chords; voicings rarely changed unless a new section was presented in the song.

Ex. 4

Track 3

Certain organists, such as Booker T. Jones from the Stax record label, began to redefine the role of the organ in R&B soul music. It wasn't long before every band wanted the pianist to play the organ as well. R&B soul keyboard players like Sly and Rose Stone (from Sly & The Family Stone) revolutionized organ playing: it got stronger, borrowing more from the contemporary black gospel of the mid-to-late '60s; rhythms became louder and even more syncopated, and staccato R.H. and ghosted L.H. patterns were more common.

Ex.5

Track 3
(cont'd)

Electric Piano, Clavinet, and Harpsichord

R&B soul keyboard players from the Motown label – including Ivory Joe Hunter, Earl Van Dyke, Marvin Gaye, and Stevie Wonder – were starting to add electric pianos, clavichords, and even harpsichords into the music. Electric pianos were used to rhythmically emulate acoustic piano parts, and the clavichord was used to emulate the organ's improvised rhythms. Motown's use of the harpsichord took the music in a different direction. The harpsichord played primarily eighth-note and 16th-note patterns borrowed from classical piano.

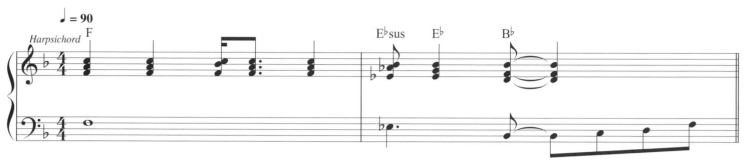

THE 1970s

R&B soul keyboard players from the early-to-mid-1970s continued to use the rhythms and instruments established during the late '60s. The increasing demands made of keyboard players at this time produced the concept of the multi-keyboardist, a player who was expected to perform on at least two keyboard instruments.

The Fender Rhodes piano had a distinguishable sound and rhythm. The concept of pads was also employed during this era. The whole-note-sustaining Rhodes sound used by Stevie Wonder, Billy Beck, Walter "Junie" Morrison, and Larry Dunn spoke to a generation.

The Monophonic Synthesizer and the String Machine

Other R&B soul keyboard players from the mid-to-late-'70s began to use the Minimoog synthesizer. Since this instrument played only one note at a time, the keyboard player used it either to play lead-line melodies, solo, or to create strange sound effects. Because this instrument was capable of bending notes, many R&B soul keyboard players utilized it to play simulated guitar and horn parts. Other types of synthesizers created during this period, like the Arp Odyssey, Arp String Ensemble, and the Mellotron (possibly the first version of a sampling keyboard) employed just about every imaginable type of rhythm. Certain R&B soul keyboard players – Herbie Hancock, Larry Dunn, Stevie Wonder, Billy Beck, Bernie Worrell, Walter "Junie" Morrison, Milan Williams, et al. – helped define the retro-styled keyboard playing that became popular again in the late 1990s. This style of playing led the way for keyboard players to become an invaluable part of the rhythm section.

Ex. 8

Track 5

THE 1980s AND THE POLYPHONIC SYNTHESIZER

At the start of the 1980s, R&B soul keyboard playing took a turn. Polyphonic synthesizers such as the Sequential Prophet 5, Yamaha CS1, Oberheim OB8, and others began to turn up on R&B soul recordings and even on stage. These instruments revolutionized the way keyboards were used. Many of the syncopated, organ-like rhythms that appeared in the '60s and '70s were being explored. Polysynths made it easier to play 16th-note horn lines and second guitar parts on keyboard. With polyphony, R&B soul keyboardists could bend and glide whole chords, creating everything from sonic walls of sound to tight, square-wave, buzzie-sounding rhythmic funk lines. R&B soul keyboard players – including Prince, Jimmy Jam, Leon Sylvers, Norman Beavers, Kashif, et al. – began to expand on traditional R&B soul rhythms. These players added new rhythms such as horn stabs on beat 2, 16th-note chords, pitch and mod wheel downbeat accents, black-key and white-key glisses with pedal sustain, and many more.

Ex. 9

Track 5
(cont'd)

THE 1990s AND THE SAMPLING KEYBOARD

During the late 1980s and early 1990s, the sampling keyboard became a big part of R&B soul keyboard playing. There were still players who continued to use the sounds and techniques employed by traditional R&B, but many keyboardists abandoned much of the rhythm and articulation commonly found in R&B. Some chose to change to a stripped-down, generic version of R&B; others almost exclusively used samplers, along with samples of older R&B songs and grooves. Many opted for samples of ambience, LP-record scratch noises, vocal sounds, etc. with loose rhythms and multi-dimensional rhythmic concepts found in modern rap and hip-hop.

Ex. 10: Rap/Hip-Hop

Track 6

In this book, we primarily will study the R&B soul styles made popular from the late 1950s through the late 1970s. This is R&B soul at its finest. If you can play this music with authority, playing commensurate styles such as disco, funk, rap, and hip-hop should not be difficult. It will be much easier than trying to play them without first being exposed to R&B soul keyboard playing.

Understanding R&B soul rhythm is important, but making musical choices and knowing when to make them has everything to do with your comprehension of *feel*.

FEEL

To fully absorb R&B soul keyboard playing, you must develop a good sense of *feel*. Feel refers to three aspects of playing. The first relates to exactly how a rhythm, harmony, or melody is placed within the pulse or beat of the song. In R&B soul music, feel can be interpreted as either behind the pulse, exactly on top of the pulse, or slightly ahead of the pulse. In most styles of music, the drummer usually has the job of establishing this pulse and maintaining it throughout the song.

In R&B soul music, each rhythm section player – including the keyboardist – routinely sets and maintains this for him or herself. In fact, many times the keyboard plays with a different feel than others in the band.

The second aspect of feel is harmonic, rhythmic, and melodic interplay, and role playing within an R&B soul song. Many times this is related only to a common understanding of licks. A *lick* is a melodic phrase used as an improvised pattern different from patterns of the song itself. In blues and R&B soul, licks are often copied and used in other songs. This interplay and role playing is more communicative and spontaneous than a mere contrived lick. A saxophone player interacting with a lead vocalist almost intuitively while the singer is improvising a melody is a good example. Another example is when the bass player is riffing on a melodic or rhythmic pattern almost instinctively while the drummer plays a complementary pattern. In this scenario, both musicians demonstrate an attribute of feel. The R&B soul keyboardist must be able to act and react appropriately with every other person in the rhythm section and with the vocalists. Keyboard players should know where to put an organ lick, exactly the perfect spot for a R.H. trill, when to be dynamic, and how long to hold a string sustain. This aspect of feel can be obtained only with careful attention to the music and with experience.

The third aspect of feel – *attitude* – relates to the harmonic, rhythmic, and melodic elements already present in the R&B soul song itself. No one can teach you attitude, but it is an integral part of R&B soul. There is no way Pat Boone can really sing heavy metal music. He just doesn't possess the right attitude. You can learn attitude by exposing yourself to the R&B soul experience, along with the people who understand this music. Years ago people said, "If you want to sing gospel music, you've got to visit a black church." There is a great deal of validity to that statement. How can an actor play a role effectively if he or she is not committed to each line in the script? R&B soul lyrics speak of conditions and situations that many people can identify with. If you cannot relate to the songs with a heartfelt emotion of your own, your playing will be missing one ingredient: Soul.

Feels Throughout the Eras of R&B Soul

R&B soul keyboard music can be described in five basic aspects of feel:

- Loose and laid back ('50s doo wop, '60s Stax, '70s soul)
- Tight and on top ('50s gospel, '60s Brown, '80s Prince, '70s funk)
- Syncopated and aggressive, but laid back ('50s jump blues, '60s Sly, '90s hip-hop)
- Tight and smooth ('60s Motown, '70s Philly soul)
- Loose, but aggressive ('60s rock, '70s P-Funk, '90s rap)

Many R&B soul keyboard players varied their feel from song to song and era to era. These categories should be seen in context and understood as nothing more than a musical guide for the evolution of various R&B soul feels. You must also understand that other feels more commonly associated with jazz, reggae, rock 'n' roll, and other styles have been used in R&B soul music.

THE GROOVE

Groove in R&B soul music is at the core of the style itself. Early R&B soul derived this from blues and even from big band stylings. Several distinguishable types of groove concepts eventually developed, making R&B soul a most popular sound during the 1960s. The groove contains not only the previous two elements of rhythm and feel, but also three additional important components: chord progressions, cadences, and the song form itself. It is critical to the melodic and rhythmic structure of the song that these move in an organized fashion and be interpreted correctly. It is important to the dynamic aspects of the song that a chord progression resolves effectively. Emphasis must be placed on chord resolutions or releases within the song, as they relate to the lyrics. R&B soul keyboard players should find these resolution points and interpret them musically, adding the necessary feel and groove to play with soul. In other words, if the song needs more movement in the voicing of chords within the progression, the keyboard player needs to take those liberties and adjust.

GROOVE OR MOVE?

A *cadence* is a succession of chords or rhythms that progresses in an orderly fashion from one chord or rhythm to the next. Traditionally, R&B soul music has deliberate cadences and resolutions. R&B soul keyboard players must play within these boundaries and support the song's natural progression, not fight stylistically against it. In other words, we don't want to play with the wrong feel, attitude, rhythm, or concept of the flow of the song. Keep in mind that R&B soul music has a perpetual quality to it. It seems to always be moving ahead and should be played with confidence, not holding back the groove from its forward motion.

R&B SONG FORM

R&B soul song form brings all the described concepts together. It has seen many changes over the years, but there are points of continuity. Ordinarily, songs have introductions, verses, choruses, bridges, and outros or endings. The songwriter or arranger decides exactly where or when these events happen in the song. The R&B soul songs of the late '50s had a musical intro, verses with stops, a chorus, a bridge, and a musical ending. The R&B soul songs of much of the '60s contained primarily the same form, except for endings that faded with vamps or choruses. Additionally, instrumental recordings, which became popular during that era, had varying song forms. During the '70s, the R&B soul songs usually displayed expanded intros, choruses, and included breakdowns. These breakdowns typically had drums, vocal chants, percussion, and bass.

R&B soul keyboard players need to be flexible, capable of changing roles within the context of a song's form. For example, an R&B soul keyboard part could potentially contain piano, horn, strings, organ, and even bass parts to which the keyboard player should apply concepts of rhythm, feel, and groove. Of course, we knew the job would be dangerous when we took it!

To understand R&B soul rhythm, feel, and the groove, we will go to the inception of the style: the blues. Blues keyboard playing is the unquestionable parent of R&B soul keyboard playing, so its examination is logical. In the next chapter, we will look at several forms of blues progressions, rhythms, and licks.

CHAPTER 2
THE BLUES

Blues piano played an important role in the creation of early R&B soul keyboard playing. The Mississippi delta region produced many pianists who defined the now-famed New-Orleans-style playing. This region also turned out countless renowned blues artists, including Muddy Waters, Howlin' Wolf, and B.B. King. As stated earlier, blues pianists like Otis Span migrated from the South into northern cities such as St. Louis, Chicago, Detroit, Philadelphia, and New York in search of factory work. Around this time, the advent of the electric guitar added an edge to the blues, and keyboardists had to adapt by playing harder rhythms and stronger trills to be heard over the guitar and drums. Some pianists also played organ to compensate for the new musical environment.

The blues is a genre that warrants a great deal of study on its own. It's a unique style characterized by distinct rhythms, chord patterns, scales, and riffs. To reach a fundamental understanding of the blues, let's look at some general blues concepts.

Several types of rhythmic and harmonic patterns characterize the blues. These can be eight-bar, 16-bar, 12-bar, or various other forms. The blues can be played with a straight feel, shuffle feel, boogie feel, or triplet feel. In this chapter, we will only skim the surface of all the subtleties and complexities of blues keyboards. Continue your study of blues piano playing through the many other books, videos, and recordings on the subject. For clarity, will these examples will be demonstrated in the key of C, but you should practice these patterns, scales, and harmonies in all 12 keys. Primarily, we'll demonstrate the blues using the 12-bar form and either shuffle or triplet feel.

BLUES SHUFFLE PATTERN

The blues shuffle pattern is probably the most common rhythm in blues and early R&B soul piano. This pattern is most easily understood as a triplet with the second of each three notes as a rest. Many early R&B artists – Bobby Bland, for example – used these rhythms.

 Ex. 1
Track 7

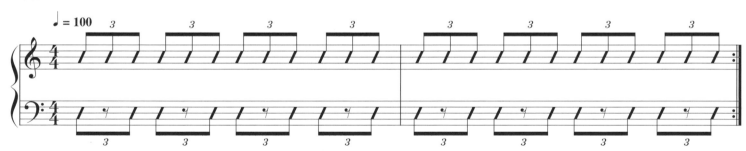

THE TRIPLET PATTERN

The triplet pattern is also quite standard and customarily is played by the pianist in blues and early R&B soul keyboards. Fats Domino made this type of rhythm popular. This feel can be notated several different ways. You may even see triplet feels notated as a dotted eighth note followed by a 16th note, as in Ex. 2.

 Ex.2
Track 7
(cont'd)

Though technically this rhythm should be written as a quarter note and an eighth note with a triplet bracket above, throughout this book (and in many manuscripts you will come across) it will be stated at the top of each figure, next to the tempo marking (♫ = ♩♪), and will appear as two eighth notes.

Ex.3

Track 7
(cont'd)

In the following example, listen as the L.H. performs the shuffle pattern and the R.H. performs the triplet pattern.

Ex. 4

Track 8

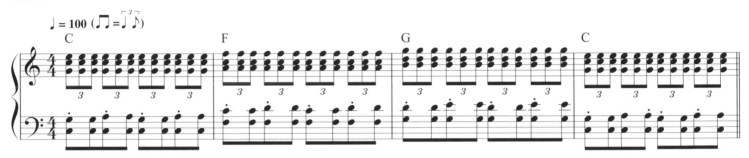

BLUES HARMONY

Essentially, blues harmony is created from the I, IV, and V chords within the major scale, adding a seventh above: I7, IV7, V7. This type of harmony is unmistakably bluesy.

Ex.5

Track 8
(cont'd)

The most common blues form using these chords is the *12-bar blues*.

Ex. 6: 12-Bar Blues Pattern (P)

Track 9

BLUES MELODY

Blues melodies are composed from either the major pentatonic scale (Ex. 7) or the blues scale (Ex. 8). These two scales are the ones most commonly used in the blues. Typically, melodies are created by using variations of the blues and major pentatonic scales on the I chord and the blues scale only on the IV and V chords. Practice these scales routinely and phase them into your soloing or improvisations over time.

 Ex. 7

Track 10

 Ex.8

Track 10
(cont'd)

Here are a few blues licks fashioned primarily from the previous two scales:

 Ex. 9 (P)

Track 11

BLUES TECHNIQUES

The *black key slide* is the most distinguishable technique of blues piano. You can apply this simply by sliding the same finger from a black key into a white one. It can be used with single-note melodies or even when playing chords.

The *double stop* is another typical device used in both blues and R&B soul keyboards. This occurs when you play two notes at the same time within a blues improvisation. It was originally thought of as an imitation of a blues guitar riff.

Ex. 10: Double Stops (P)

Track 12

The use of the *trill* or *tremolo* is also common in both blues and R&B soul keyboard playing. Do this by using either third or sixth intervals. These should be trilled by the R.H. – shaken vigorously from left to right and moved and inverted – while maintaining the L.H. shuffle pattern.

Ex. 11: Trill Pattern (P)

Track 13

There are many other blues characteristics that became common with keyboard playing. Some of these include the gliss, the roll, stride, boogie woogie, and crushed-note techniques. It would be worth your time and effort to study blues keyboard methods and instructional books to become more familiar with these.

THE DIFFERENCE BETWEEN R&B AND BLUES

R&B soul keyboards that became popular in the 1950s evolved from variations of these blues piano playing techniques. Chronologically speaking, the blues was created first. It was an extremely raw, primal form of music that rose out of the South. The lyrics spoke of vice, infidelity, crudeness, humor, and rebellious attitudes. The feel was loose and free, and the song form varied from section to section. African-Americans were the primary practitioners of this music.

R&B soul music was created in the 1940s and '50s and can be seen as an electrified and slightly refined version of the blues. The lyrics contained suggestive references to vice, infidelity, loving relationships, humor, dancing, singing, and rebellious attitudes. The feel was aggressive, and the song form varied, but became more structured in the '50s. African-Americans were the primary practitioners of this music. (Gospel music played an important role in the creation of R&B soul music. We will examine this relationship in Chapter 3.)

THE DIFFERENCE BETWEEN R&B AND ROCK 'N' ROLL

Rock 'n' roll piano style had its roots in early blues piano as well. In fact, the differences between blues, R&B, and rock 'n' roll music during the '50s dealt primarily with factors of region, lyrics, feel, and the race of those who played these types of music.

Rock 'n' roll music was created in the '50s and can be thought of as an electrified and slightly refined version of R&B soul music. Although the music was popular with the youth, mainstream airwaves did not support this music because it was believed to be too black for white kids. Needless to say, early rock 'n' roll found minimal airplay. This music was played mostly at high school hops and in the homes of the teens themselves. The lyrics of rock 'n' roll recordings contained suggestive references to vice, infidelity, loving relationships, humor, dancing, singing, and rebellious attitudes. The feel was aggressive and loud. The song form was an imitation of R&B soul song form, but began to become more distinctly structured by the late '50s. Caucasians and African-Americans were the primary practitioners of this music.

There are many instructional books, videos, and biographies that explain the relationship between blues, R&B, and rock 'n' roll. Obtain these books and continue to study the differences and the history of how rock 'n' roll music evolved into more modern styles like rock, metal, pop, and grunge.

CHAPTER 3

GOSPEL AND SOUL KEYBOARD VOICINGS

Soul keyboard playing was profoundly influenced by gospel piano and organ techniques. Many of these can be heard in the recordings of Motown artists and musicians from the early 1960s. In this chapter, we will learn several gospel keyboard patterns and procedures and compare them with those found in soul keyboards.

Black gospel music was different from the style of traditional white gospel hymns. The most noticeable disparity was that black Baptist and Pentecostal churches had percussion, rhythm, dancing, and shouting. Frequently, the musical ensemble included full rhythm sections instead of just a pianist or organist (as was the norm for white churches and cathedrals). The black gospel churches regularly used syncopated rhythms and full choirs, whereas the white churches kept their musical arrangements more reserved, rarely deviating from post-classical convention. In black gospel churches, even the ministers themselves got involved with the action by singing their sermons rather than offering mundane recitations or speeches. The church's worship service was more like entertainment.

Gospel music song form has many similarities with that of soul music. Gospel music usually has an introduction, several verses, a chorus with refrain that includes a choir or background accompaniment, and a chorus vamp with accompaniment. The lead vocalist almost always starts and ends the song with expressive improvisations.

Soul keyboard players like Ray Charles, Aretha Franklin, and Billy Preston contributed substantially to this style by redefining how the piano and organ could be used in soul music. They ingeniously merged common gospel rhythms and melodies into their own songs to set a new path into motion.

GOSPEL HARMONY

Gospel music uses the major scale for its main chord structures, centering around the I, IV, and V chords, similar to blues. Gospel music's use of passing chords distinguishes it from the blues. Also, as these chords pass from one to the next, the bass notes do not always reflect the root of each chord. The strong beats of a rhythm or even a cadence can contain pedal-point bass lines.

Gospel piano uses the major chord as the primary key center; the minor chord is used as the secondary key center, the dominant 7th chord is used at the end of a harmonic cadence, and the diminished chord is used in passing from one chord to another.

 Ex. 1: Gospel Progression

In gospel harmony, the major and minor chord can be substituted for one another when the chord is moving in and out of a harmonic resolution or during a rhythmic cadence. This gives the harmony a blues-like sound because of the interchange between the major and minor third of each chord.

Ex. 2: Minor-Major Lick

Track 14
(cont'd)

GOSPEL INTRODUCTIONS

As stated earlier, gospel music starts with a musical intro that sets up the feel, tempo, meter, and mood of the song. The song form, along with the resolution of the harmonic cadence, most often dictates that a dominant chord be used to lead the vocalist correctly into the song.

Ex. 3: Gospel Intro 1 (P)

Track 15

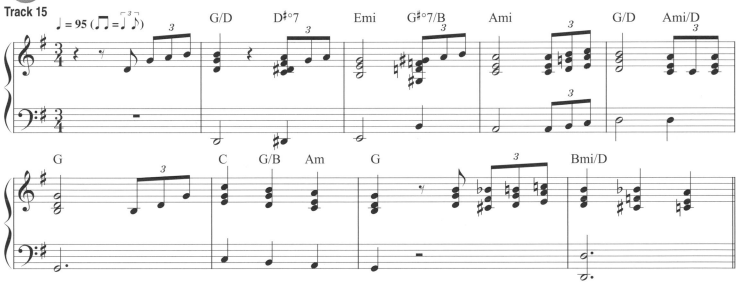

Ex. 4: Gospel Intro 2

Track 15
(cont'd)

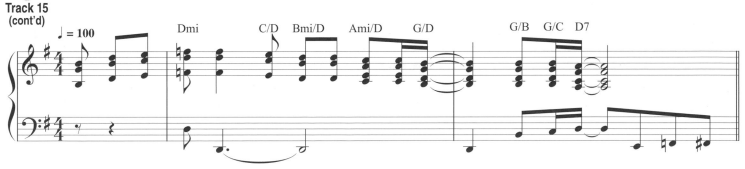

Ex. 5: Gospel Intro 3

Track 15
(cont'd)

GOSPEL RHYTHM

Gospel rhythms revolve primarily around syncopation. This is noticeable in any aspect of the keyboard parts: the piano L.H. bass can contain syncopation along with R.H. chords and melodies. This makes keeping a steady beat more difficult. It also provides a significant challenge to your L.H. and R.H. coordination. In rising to this challenge, you will develop good independence abilities, which can help considerably with multiple-part playing. We will examine this in more detail in Chapters 9 and 10.

Ex. 6: L.H. and R.H. Syncopation

Track 16

Gospel rhythm generally has a fast-paced eighth-note feel with an emphasis on the "and" of each beat. Because of this, the feel becomes rather syncopated. Many soul R&B artists, like Sly & The Family Stone, utilized this type of feel and created new concepts in soul music.

Ex. 7: Gospel Groove

Track 17

Gospel music frequently calls for 6/8, 12/8, and 3/4 meter, along with triplet figures. When these patterns are used within gospel song structure, syncopation is achieved. The pulse is centered on the downbeat. Additionally, an accent is placed on the third 16th-note triplet of beat 6 within the 6/8 meter.

Ex. 8: Gospel Triplet Feel

Track 18

The gospel piano player is free within this type of rhythm to accent any of the weak or strong beats. The pianist can also invert chords, play quarter-, eighth-, or 16th-note triplets with rests, ties, or any other variations. This type of playing became prevalent in '60s soul music.

Ex. 9: Free Triplet Chord Pattern

Track 19

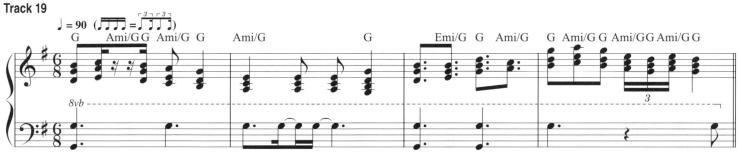

GOSPEL PIANO TECHNIQUES

Octaves are an important device when performing gospel piano music. Gospel pianists use octaves when playing chords, rhythms, and especially melodies and improvisations.

Ex. 10: Octave Pattern (P)

Track 20

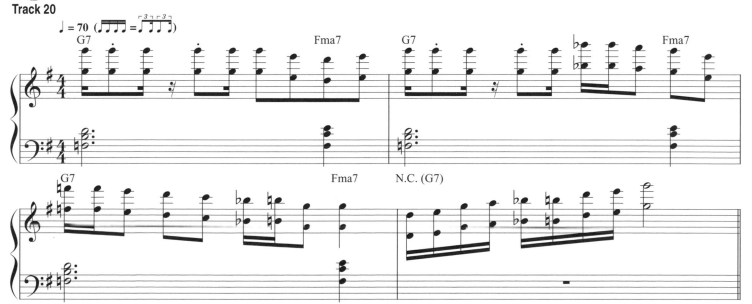

Grace notes and double or triple stops are also a notable part of the style. They are often applied within the progression of the chord harmony.

Ex. 11: Grace Note Pattern

Track 21

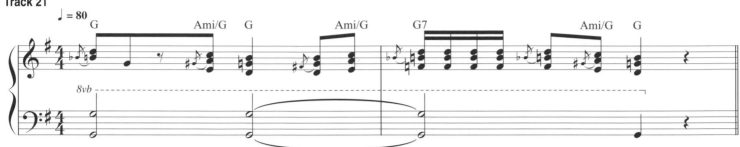

Dynamics are a crucial aspect in playing both gospel and soul keyboard parts. Soul music is quite emotional, so the dynamics include both highs and lows. The lyrics and song form are usually the deciding factors as to how and when the dynamics should occur.

Ex. 12: Dynamic Pattern

Track 22

Using L.H. octaves with pedal sustain is another gospel piano technique. This should occur when moving chords back and forth with the R.H.

Ex. 13: L.H. Pedal Point

Track 23

The practice of inverting chords is found in all styles, but its frequency in gospel piano makes it stylistically unique. Again, syncopation during chord inversions adds to the effectiveness of this type of voicing.

Ex. 14: Gospel Groove 2 (P)

Track 24

Ex. 15: Gospel Groove 3 (P)

Track 24
(cont'd)

Using a *roll* to strike chords is common within gospel music. This articulation is easily identifiable, even in other styles of music.

Those keyboard players interested in furthering their investigation of gospel music are encouraged to listen closely to gospel piano recordings and learn from any available books, CDs, and online videos. As stated in the previous chapter, learning a new style requires a great deal of study and practice. This book is designed to provide you with introductory instruction and exercises. The gospel and soul keyboard concepts and ideas explored here are only the tip of the iceberg.

THE DIFFERENCE BETWEEN R&B AND SOUL KEYBOARDS

The difference between R&B and soul keyboards is basically this: R&B is rough, and soul is smooth. R&B is hard-driving, raw, and rough. James Brown, Wilson Pickett, Al Green, and Otis Redding are R&B singers. Booker T. Jones, Earl Van Dyke, Leroy Flick Hodges, and Ivory Joe Hunter are R&B keyboard players. R&B is basic in its harmony, rhythm, and song structure. R&B lyrics are most often clever stories that use parody, metaphor, and humor to convey the ideas explained in Chapter 2.

Soul music is laid-back, emotional, and smooth. Aretha Franklin, Curtis Mayfield, Marvin Gaye, Chaka Khan, Stephanie Mills, and Luther Vandross are soul singers. Aretha Franklin, Donny Hathaway, Stevie Wonder, and Richard Tee are soul keyboard players. Soul music, harmony, and structure has progressed into greater musical complexities, borrowing rhythms and harmonies from jazz and African music. Artists such as Earth, Wind & Fire, Parliament, Donny Hathaway, and Stevie Wonder created innovative concepts in the 1970s to forge a new path.

As stated earlier, the lyrics of a soul song generally dictate its dynamic range. Soul lyrics can be about relationships, obsession, environment, social conditions, or everyday life. They are similar to R&B, with the inclusion of spiritual messages. Soul lyrics are rarely derogatory, nor do they contain references to vice or rebellious attitudes. Instead, they deal with the expression of feelings about love and life, and generally tend to follow the sacred spiritual tradition, so it's no wonder that soul keyboard playing can often be a spiritual experience!

CHAPTER 4
TECHNIQUE, INDEPENDENCE, AND THE LEFT HAND

Technique normally implies correct physical procedures for playing the keyboard. For example, in classical music, the pianist uses specific fingerings to play certain melodies and chords. When similar melodies and chords recur, the pianist can resort to the same fingerings to play them with good technique. While this may be true for classical music, it is only half true in R&B soul music. You certainly need technical know-how to play R&B soul keyboards, but you must also learn new approaches. Because of the improvisational nature of this style, it is necessary to become versatile and perhaps absorb several ways of accomplishing the same thing.

If you were classically trained, you might have learned never to use the thumb on a black key. Your idea of music theory may also consist of numerous rules that should never be broken. In R&B soul music, many of these are purposely ignored. As a reference, the standard fingerings for the 12 major scales are given below. It is important to note that, although these are standard fingerings, they can be varied for different purposes – to suit the size of your hand, to employ unorthodox procedures, etc. Remain flexible in your attitude about R&B soul keyboard facility, and recognize that rules are made to be broken.

Ex. 1: C Major Scale (P)

Track 25

Ex. 2: D Major Scale

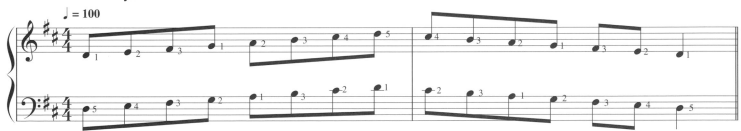

Ex. 3: E Major Scale

Ex. 4: G Major Scale

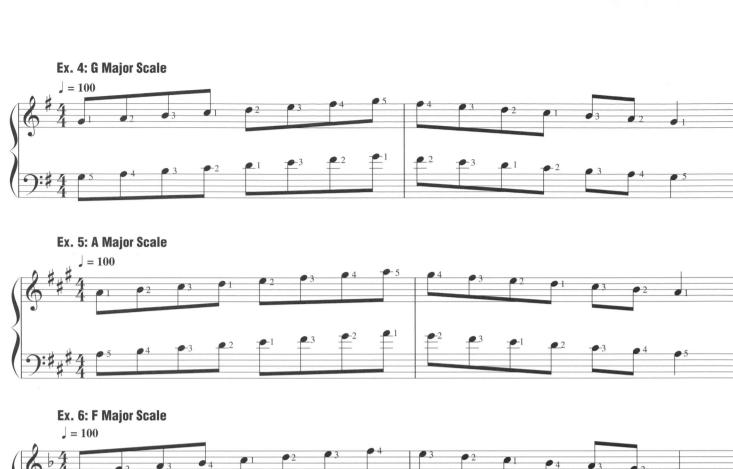

Ex. 5: A Major Scale

Ex. 6: F Major Scale

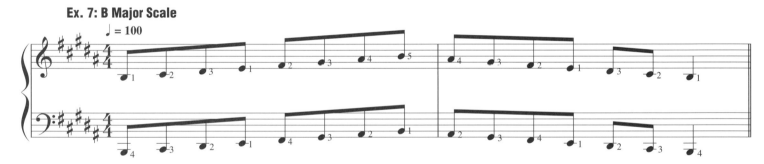

Ex. 7: B Major Scale

Ex. 8: D♭ Major Scale

Ex. 9: A♭ Major Scale

Ex. 10: E♭ Major Scale

Ex. 11: B♭ Major Scale

Ex. 12: G♭ Major Scale

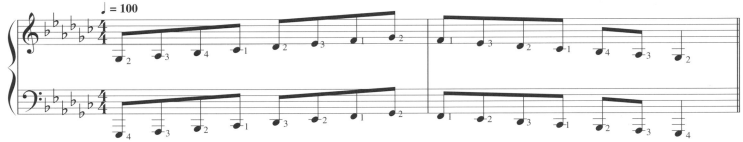

RIGHT-HAND PRIORITY VOICE LEADING

R&B soul keyboard concepts have developed considerably over many years. After long periods of time, various techniques like licks, voicings, and phrasing have become a part of the musical language. Playing chords with the R.H. and bass notes/lines with the L.H. is a trademark of R&B soul keyboard. This developed as piano players began compensating for not having full rhythm sections when either writing or rehearsing a song. When keyboardists perform this way, they routinely voice the R.H. chords in inversions. These inversions are easily configured for right-hand mobility. For the sake of clarity, we will call this procedure *R.H. priority voice leading*.

Right-hand
priority voice leading

Ex. 13: R.H. Priority Voice Leading (P)

Track 26

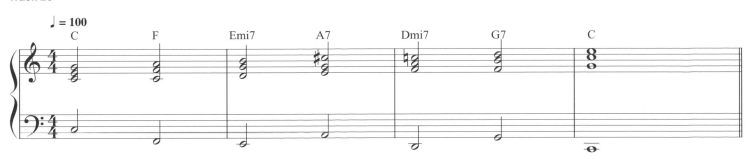

This type of playing is also common in rock, pop, and funk. Although R.H. priority voice leading is a useful method for learning and playing songs, it should by no means represent your only approach. You should also be able to play chords in the L.H. and melodies in the R.H., or enlist the L.H. or R.H. to play melodies or chords on an entirely different keyboard, if necessary. R&B soul keyboard players regularly vary the way they play, from being an accompanist to being a member of the rhythm section.

INDEPENDENCE

With the introduction of gospel keyboard concepts into R&B soul keyboard, solid L.H. and R.H. independence was required. Additionally, many R&B soul artists needed pianists who could also play organ. Playing more than one instrument at the same time obviously creates some difficulties, but also makes the keyboard player a valuable, if not indispensible, member of the rhythm section. In this chapter, we present some general independence exercises. The practical application of this concept will be examined in more detail in Chapters 6, 9, and 10.

R.H. CHORD AND L.H. SHUFFLE RHYTHM

To develop reliable independence, you must first coordinate the two hands. To do this, first examine where the hands are striking together and where the L.H. or R.H. is striking alone. This may seem obvious; however, it could be one of the first things you fail to do in the midst of a problem. It is also necessary to subdivide and count all the beats and rests aloud. This becomes important when playing patterns that include 16th-note subdivisions. The following example is a shuffle rhythm with rests in the R.H. Practice this pattern routinely to help develop your coordination.

Ex. 14: Shuffle Rhythm (P)

Track 27

L.H. AND R.H. CONTRASTING TOUCH EXERCISE

As you improve your coordination, it will become more and more necessary to vary the articulation between hands. Some of these differences can be dynamics, staccato, legato, etc. The following exercise will help you with contrasting touch challenges. Pay close attention to the dynamics, articulations, and note durations.

 Ex. 15: Contrasting Touch Drill (P)

Track 28

L.H. AND R.H. TREMOLO WRIST EXERCISE

R&B soul keyboard players often play patterns that require the wrists on either hand to shimmer. This exercise is designed to cultivate the coordination necessary to effectively produce *tremolo* with either hand.

 Ex. 16: Tremolo Wrist Exercise (P)

Track 29

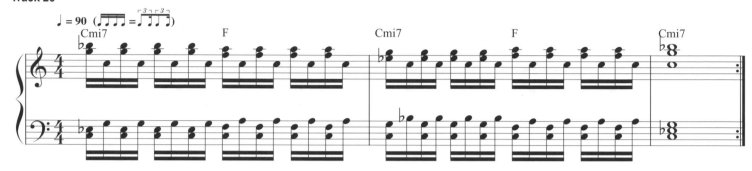

L.H. ROOT AS GHOST NOTE

The L.H. can be commissioned to ghost rhythms within a R.H. groove. This adds syncopation to keyboard parts and makes the pattern much more musically interesting.

 Ex. 17: L.H. Ghost Notes (P)

Track 30

L.H. ROLL WITH R.H. CHORD

You can use your L.H. to roll into chords played by the R.H. Many of the Motown keyboardists of the 1960s employed this technique on the popular hits of that era.

L.H. GLISS WITH R.H. CHORD

R&B soul and blues keyboard players use many procedures that are unorthodox to classical technique. Some are so unique, they help define the style itself. A short L.H. gliss followed by a R.H. chord is one of these. This can be used with a piano or organ sound. The following exercise will help you coordinate this gliss with both hands.

Ex. 18: L.H. Glissando Exercise (P)

Track 31

L.H. OCTAVE WITH R.H. CHORD

As stated earlier, gospel keyboard concepts influenced the way R&B soul keyboardists were performing in the 1960s and '70s. Playing octaves in the L.H. bass while executing syncopated chords in the R.H was one oft-used method. This became popular within funk and R&B. Again, the organ, piano, and clavinet are the proper instruments for this technique.

THE LEFT HAND

There are many other technical skills that can be used within the R&B soul keyboard style. Some of these include bass lines, stride, and shell voicing. Continue listening to various R&B soul songs to see how many more independence techniques you hear. Since most of these utilize the L.H., don't neglect it and settle for being a one-handed player. Many keyboard players fail to fully develop facility with the L.H. It requires a great deal of practice and coordination to acquire hand independence, but the end result is well worth the effort. Once you have developed a good sense of rhythm, feel, groove, voicing, and independence, you will be at a functional level of musicianship, prepared to play and even create R&B soul music. For those students who desire a greater understanding of R&B soul keyboards and are prepared for more study, stay tuned.

CHAPTER 5
PIANO, ORGAN, STRINGS, AND HORNS

CHOOSING R&B KEYBOARDS

Currently, there are hundreds of keyboards on the market and hundreds more that have been manufactured over the past 35 years. Some are monophonic, others are polyphonic. Some have on-board effects while others don't. Some have internal sequencers, others are multi-timbral. The number of choices is mind-boggling. If you are like most keyboard players, you will find it difficult to decide exactly which instrument you really need. As a teacher, the question most students as me is, "Which keyboard is the best to buy if I want to play R&B soul music?" Unfortunately, no single keyboard can possibly do all the tasks we would like it to do. If you want the answer, first ask a few more questions:

Choosing R&B keyboards

1) Is this an instrument I can grow into, and is it expandable?

2) Do I need a controller with weighted action?

3) What is the minimal number of instruments I am able to play simultaneously?

4) Will I need a sampling workstation?

5) Will I need additional modules or a home studio to record songs?

These questions are critical and could determine your ultimate investment toward your sound and career. For this reason, I routinely offer the following advice:

1) If you are going to become a professional R&B soul keyboard player, you should prepare to purchase two keyboards and at least one module. One keyboard should be a weighted controller capable of providing great electric and acoustic piano sounds and should have at least 76 keys. The other keyboard should be a non-weighted multi-timbral synthesizer capable of simulating many hybrid and synthetic sounds and should have at least 61 keys. The module should be some sort of sampler, so you can achieve any sound effect or authentic acoustic sound. R&B soul music traditionally requires the keyboard player to have instruments that can simulate piano, organ, string, and horn sounds effectively, and often simultaneously. Contemporary R&B soul music demands even more. There is no way one keyboard, especially the $100-$200 home or portable type keyboards, can convincingly replicate these sounds. They generally have inferior sounds, built-in cheesy rhythm machines, and weak built-in speakers. Many times these keyboards don't have external outputs and may not even have standard-size keys. If you already own one of these keyboards, you should realize that, although they may be adequate to learn on, they are not designed for the professional. You've found a bargain when you purchase what you really need. Remember: "You get what you pay for."

2) R&B soul keyboard players should educate themselves on all the elements of music: harmony, melody, rhythm, and tonality. To understand these, we must also understand the language of music. We need to be taught a way to communicate with those who have obtained levels of mastery in music. To that end, it would be helpful to learn to read music, learn musical terminology, and study composers to join the world of musicianship already established for us. This global community has been maintained for thousands of years by many talented minds. Most beginning keyboard players are intimidated by this idea and feel bad because they don't know as much about music as those talented people do. What they often forget is that every keyboardist who ever played had to start from the same place that he/she is currently starting

from. Beginners should look at professionals to get an accurate and inspiring perception of what it takes to be great and just how great they too can be.

Many potential keyboard players are in such a hurry to start playing music and writing songs that they never achieve a functional level of proficiency with these essential elements. The excitement of getting an instrument often turns to frustration and apathy because the beginner loses sight of a few little things. It takes hard work, talent, and time to be a great player. Many times, we forget that playing the keyboard is a skill that doesn't get fully developed without dedication, persistence, patience, and practice. There is no substitute for this.

In this age of technology, we sometimes fail to remember that these instruments can't really play themselves and certainly they cannot play anything great without the creative minds that program them.

3) Every modern R&B soul keyboard player should acquire a functional level of knowledge and facility about MIDI and MIDI applications such as sequencing, effects, and data storage. Contemporary R&B soul keyboard players are increasingly having to apply MIDI functions to live performances as well as recording situations, including syncing sequenced patterns to DAT machines, SMPTE boxes, and drum machines or recording to multitrack recorders or computers. Learning about MIDI can make many of your tasks as an R&B soul keyboard player much simpler. If you have a keyboard with an integrated sequencer or if you have a computer-based sequencer, take the necessary time to learn it thoroughly.

UNDERSTANDING THE ROLE OF THE KEYBOARD

The role of the R&B soul keyboard player has changed over time, but significantly so in recent decades. There was a period during the 1970s when an R&B soul keyboard player needed to bring only a Fender Rhodes piano, a Hammond or Farfisa organ, and perhaps a string machine to a gig; he'd have more than enough sounds to please the band. If you survived carrying either the Hammond or the Rhodes up flights of stairs and through hotel kitchens, then at least you would sound good! Throughout the 1980s, R&B soul keyboard players needed at least a great piano sound and a polyphonic synthesizer, which could simulate brass, organ, strings, and bells. The keyboard player no longer had to worry about lugging heavy keyboards around, but substituted that chore for the terror of switching patches between songs or often during songs. The 1990s provided R&B soul keyboardists much more ease of operation: keyboards with computerized touch panels, larger data windows, on-board effects, and many more contemporary features. Now the keyboard player's Fender Rhodes or Hammond organ sound can be stored in the form of a cartridge small enough to carry in your pocket. The dilemma for the modern keyboard player is how to afford these high-priced instruments and related equipment.

There used to be a time when a keyboard player could work with a band long enough to afford the gear he/she needed. In fact, if you were lucky, perhaps the band would collectively buy the keyboards you needed. Nowadays, keyboard players are often selected to be in bands because of the great keyboards they already own.

The R&B soul keyboard player must fulfill various roles in the context of an R&B soul band. They must provide accompaniment for the vocalist or even an instrumental soloist, they must orchestrate R&B soul music arrangements (with horns, strings, etc.), they must provide rhythm patterns that lock with guitar players and drummers, they must occasionally provide bass lines, and they must provide sound effects like samples, hits, and stabs. With so many functions to fulfill, the R&B soul keyboardist must be able to change hats as frequently as several times within the same song.

To accomplish this with ease, R&B soul keyboard players must have full control over any number of aspects and parameters. They should acquire independence skills, varied articulation, dynamic mixing skills, and instrument range knowledge. A great ear wouldn't hurt, either.

Let's be pragmatic and focus on the sounds most commonly associated with R&B keyboards. Obviously, R&B soul keyboard players need to have an understanding of various aspects of other sounds, but for the purpose of this book, piano, organ, strings, and horn concepts will be examined.

ASDR – ATTACK, SUSTAIN, DECAY, AND RELEASE

The piano, organ, strings, and horns each have singularly different attacks, sustains, decays, and releases. Because of this, you cannot articulate the piano the same way you articulate strings, for example. This articulation can also change from song to song for an individual instrument. For instance, the piano in a ballad should be sustained differently than in a hard R&B dance song. The following audio examples demonstrate how to articulate a part correctly, based on the unique way the instrument should be phrased.

Ex. 1: Piano Articulation Exercise 1

Track 32

Ex. 2: Piano Articulation Exercise 2

Track 32
(cont'd)

Ex. 3: Piano Articulation Exercise 3 (P)

Track 33

Ex. 4: Organ Articulation Exercise 1

Track 34

 Ex. 5: Organ Articulation Exercise 2

Track 34
(cont'd)

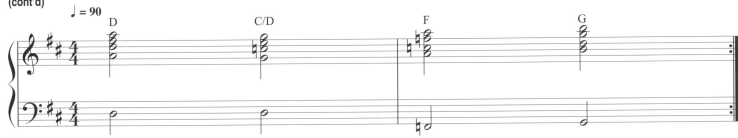

 Ex. 6: Organ Articulation Exercise 3 (P)

Track 35

 Ex. 7: String Articulation Exercise 1 (P)

Track 36

 Ex. 8: String Articulation Exercise 2 (P)

Track 37

Ex. 9: String Articulation Exercise 3 (P)

Track 38

Ex. 10: Horn Articulation Exercise 1

Track 39

Ex. 11: Horn Articulation Exercise 2 (P)

Track 39
(cont'd)

Ex. 12: Horn Articulation Exercise 3 (P)

Track 40

BLACK KEY DYNAMICS

When you play piano, organ, string, or horn parts, you must be aware of a natural impediment regarding melodic or scale-like passages on the keyboard. This particular obstacle has to do with the black key position versus the white-key position. Traditional keyboard technique teaches us to strike each key with the same velocity when practicing scales and exercises. If you notice, the white keys are three-fourths (3/4) of an inch lower on the keyboard than the black keys. So when we strike the keys, we reach the black keys in a shorter distance than the white keys. This causes us to strike harder on the black keys. Try playing a D major scale to see if this occurs. As you play piano, organ, string, and horn parts, this disparity becomes magnified. Listen carefully to all your parts and make the necessary adjustments to play more realistic keyboard parts with either hand.

DYNAMIC MIXING OF MULTIPLE KEYBOARDS

If you play a piano and organ part together, it can become muddy and loud. R&B soul keyboard players must execute control over the dynamic range of the sounds they produce. Commonly, when this merger occurs, the organ sustains notes while the piano plays rhythms or inversions. A multi-timbral keyboard offers an easy way to simulate this combination. The keyboard plays both sounds at once with a pre-programmed mix. This can be acceptable; however, it doesn't allow for the L.H. and R.H. to play separate parts. The keyboard player might also use the organ's volume pedal to control the dynamic level.

INSTRUMENT RANGE

The R&B soul keyboardist should have a good concept of acoustic and synthesized instrument ranges. There is nothing worse than hearing a cheesy piano sound or an organ that is playing a chord too high or too low in the register. Many times, keyboard players who overuse the *R.H. priority voice leading* concept play L.H. bass notes that are too muddy and interfere with the bass player's range. A string part with too many notes in it is another example of ineffective instrument range.

Ex. 13: Piano, Organ, Strings, and Horns Range

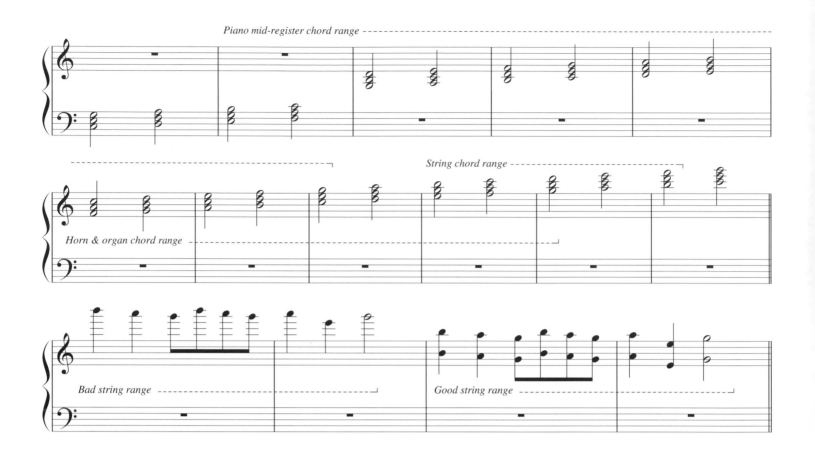

Ex. 14: Tenor and Trumpet Range

Ex. 15: Organ Range

Sometimes these range conflicts occur when the keyboard player does not know the correct frequency of the instrument being simulated. Other times, keyboardists simply play in the range or octave their L.H. or R.H. happens to be in at the current moment. You should become accustomed to quickly changing from octave to octave, as necessary. In addition, choose instrumental sounds wisely. Obviously, if you use a sampler with an eight-bit sample rate or if your polyphony is minimal, the result will be a bad sound. Listen and compare.

Occasionally, the sonic environment is not suitable for a chosen sound: There are times when the acoustics in the room don't allow a series of harmonics to be clearly audible. When this occurs, you may need to re-harmonize or invert chords. This is another good reason to engage in daily ear-training exercises.

AMPLIFICATION

R&B soul keyboard players need good amplification for their instruments. This can be interpreted differently for live or home settings. If you play live and on more than one keyboard, you should use a stereo mixer with at least a parametric EQ, effects, and auxiliary sends. You'll also want a monitor send for on-stage monitoring. A non-powered mixer with a separate power amp in order to cut down on noise is also a good idea. Use a single 15-inch speaker with horn and tweeter to amplify your mix. Many modern R&B soul keyboard players employ large stereo studio monitors mounted at ear level on stage for individual amplification. This is a solid plan, because you can hear the full stereo spectrum, along with customized mixes of other instruments on stage fed directly to your monitor mix.

ON-BOARD EFFECTS

As stated earlier, many polyphonic keyboards have effects such as chorus, reverb, and delay built into them. These types of keyboards make it much easier to authentically simulate piano, organ, strings, or horns. Without these on-board effects, you would have to buy separate outboard effects processors just for your keyboards.

CHAPTER 6

RHYTHM & BLUES PLAYING EXAMPLES

The basic patterns in this chapter emulate normal R&B soul grooves. However, most are limited to intros, minimal bar drills, hits, stops, turnarounds, or endings. They contain many techniques already presented in this book, including: L.H. bass, R.H. dominant chords with black-key slides; R.H. 16th-note pushes; L.H. and R.H. octaves; R.H. chromatic third melodies; two-hand syncopation patterns; R.H. gliss ascending/descending; two-, four-, eight-, and 12-bar grooves; turnarounds; and endings.

L.H. Bass and R.H. Dominant Chords with Black Key Slides

Ex. 1: L.H. Bass w/R.H. Chord Exercise (P)

Track 41

R.H. 16th-Note Push Patterns

Ex. 2: 16th-Note Push Drill 1 (P)

Track 42

Ex. 3: 16th-Note Push Drill 2 (P)

Track 43

Ex. 4: 16th-Note Push Drill 3 (P)

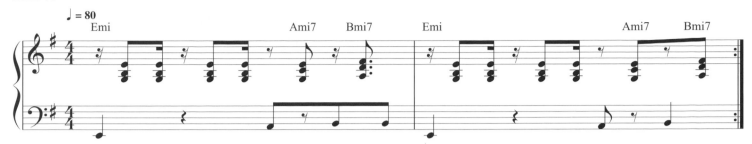

More Independence Drills

In these examples, there are a couple of one-bar patterns that will help prepare you for Chapters 9 and 10. These are syncopated and represent straight 16th notes and triplet-feel syncopation, which are prevalent in funk.

Ex. 5: Syncopated 16th-Note Drill (P)

Ex. 6: Triplet Drill (P)

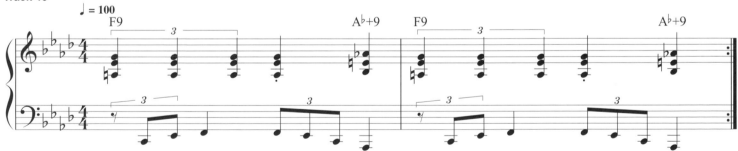

L.H. and R.H. Octave Patterns

As we studied in Chapter 3, octaves play an important role in gospel-styled soul keyboard playing. You can gain facility with the following expansion techniques, which were fashioned to help you play octaves accurately. Practice them chromatically on a daily basis.

Ex. 7: Two-Hand Octave Drill (P)

Track 47

Ex. 8: L.H. Chord and Octave Drill

Track 48

Ex. 9: R.H. Chord and Octave Drill

Track 48
(cont'd)

Two-Bar Patterns

As you play this two-bar etude, maintain the right feel by using accents and establishing a strong pulse. Listen to Track 49 for articulation and dynamics.

Ex. 10: Two-Bar Pattern (P)

Track 49

Four-Bar Patterns

Again, listen to the audio tracks to get a sense of the groove of each example.

 Ex. 11: Four-Bar Shuffle (P)

Track 50

 Ex. 12: Four-Bar Ballad (P)

Track 51

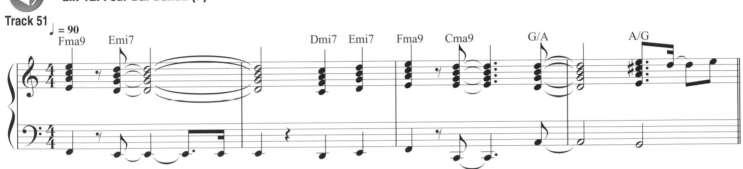

 Ex. 13: Four-Bar Funky Groove (P)

Track 52

Eight-Bar Patterns

In these eight-bar exercises, notice how different the pulse feels – compared to the previous four-bar examples.

 Ex. 14: Eight-Bar Soul Groove (P)

Track 53

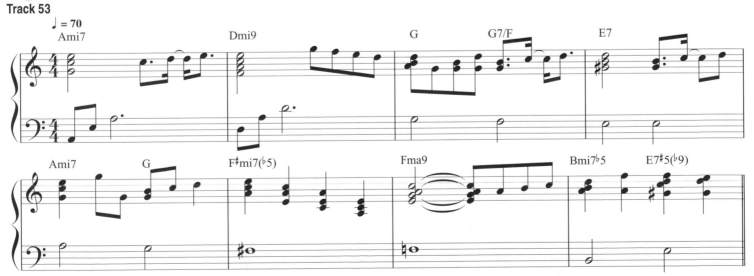

Track 54

Ex. 15: Eight-Bar R&B Shuffle Groove (P)

12-Bar Patterns

Track 55

Ex. 16: 12-Bar Minor R&B Progression (P)

Track 56

Ex. 17: 12-Bar R&B Progression

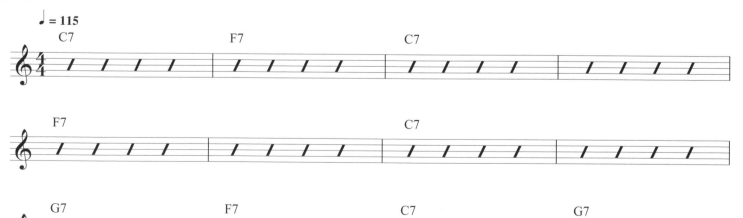

What Is a Gliss?

A *gliss* (a shortened form of the word *glissando*) is a technique that involves sliding the R.H. or L.H. up or down the white or black keys; it is often used with the sustain pedal. On most occasions, a gliss is played rapidly, but there are times when a slow gliss can be appropriate. For a descending gliss, use either the back of the L.H. or the thumb of the R.H. In either case, it is advisable to use only the fingertips; don't dig into the notes too hard or you might injure your knuckles or fingers. In the Jackson 5's "I Want You Back," you can hear a piano gliss on the white keys. Utilize the gliss when you want to create emphasis on a dynamic part of the song. For example, you might play a slow gliss on the electric piano just a beat or two before a bridge within the song structure. The black-key gliss is common in R&B soul music from the 1970s into the present.

Ex. 18: Glissando

Track 57

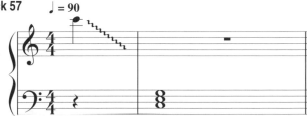

Look carefully at the following pictures to see how to properly perform a gliss. Be careful! You could hurt your hand if you play a gliss the wrong way.

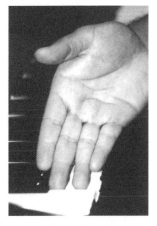

Right hand
ascending gliss

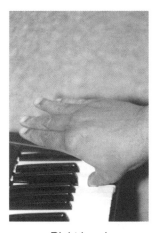

Right hand
descending gliss

Left hand
ascending gliss

Left hand
descending gliss

The Turnaround

R&B soul music has an established pattern that gets you back to the start of a progression: the turnaround. The origin of this term is simple, since its purpose is to musically "turn around" and go back to the beginning. R&B soul turnarounds are usually two-bar patterns that come at the end of a 12-bar progression, though they can be as short as one bar or even just a few beats. The early R&B of the 1950s used turnarounds quite frequently in songs that followed the blues tradition. R&B soul turnarounds became more defined and modern throughout the '60s and '70s. For the purpose of this book, we will study five different types of turnarounds.

Ex. 19: Motown Turnaround (P)

Track 58

Ex. 20: Chicago Turnaround from the V (P)

Track 59

Ex. 21: '60s Four-Bar Turnaround (P)

Track 60

Ex. 22: '70s Four-Bar Turnaround (P)

Track 61

Ex. 23: R&B Turnaround

Track 62

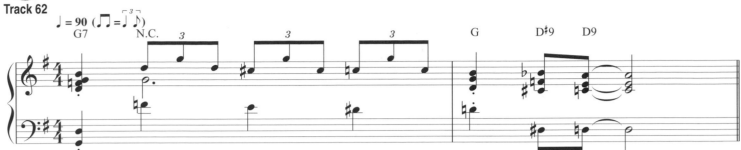

Intros

Since the intro of a piece is the first thing the audience hears, it is important that it works well to set up the mood and feel of the song. Here are two blues intros.

 Ex. 24: Blues Intro (P)

Track 63

 Ex. 25: Slow Blues (P)

Track 64

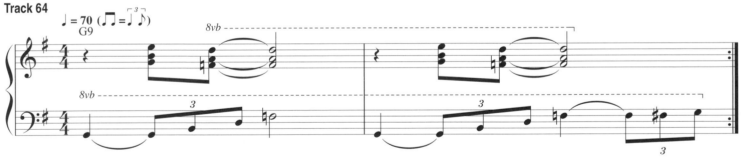

R&B Soul Endings

R&B soul music from the '50s almost always had an ending as part of the song structure; the intro of the song was often used as this ending. Routinely, the ending would employ some sort of stop time, break, or musical hit. It usually lasted a few measures and was quite musically gratifying. Other types of endings included repeating a refrain section multiple times and then stopping on beat 1 on cue. Still other types used a fermata on the last note of the song.

Ex. 26: Four-Bar Doo Wop Ending (P)

Track 65

Ex. 27: Soul Ending

Track 65
(cont'd)

Practice these drills until you are comfortable with them. Learn them in other keys to develop facility and expand your technique.

Now that you have worked on these preparatory drills, you should be ready to advance to more expressive and stylistic patterns. Those presented in the next four chapters will include enough variations to familiarize you with any R&B soul keyboard parts you may encounter in actual songs.

CHAPTER 7
SOUL GROOVES

In this chapter, we will play examples of grooves common to R&B soul keyboards. To play these patterns with the right attitude, we must listen to the artists who recorded the songs they are based on. The musicians who defined these grooves include Stevie Wonder, Marvin Gaye, Wilson Pickett, Al Green, and James Brown. (For more artists, see the Recommended Artists list at the end of the book.) A soul groove is made from the elements discussed in Chapter 1. It is important to add these new ingredients to your playing: You will need to play more than just the notes on the page. Listen carefully to how these various patterns are articulated. The drills are similar to the licks that regularly occur in R&B soul keyboards.

THE RECORD LABEL AND REGIONAL INFLUENCE

Major record companies like Chess, Motown, Hi, Epic, Stax, Atlantic, and Philadelphia International each had their own sound and interpreted R&B soul music differently. These interpretations were unique, mainly because of the diversity within regions of the United States. Chicago-style R&B soul had characteristics that distinguished it from the Memphis soul sound. Motown in Detroit had a profound influence on all R&B soul, but is by no means more soulful than Stax or Philly soul.

Listen to recordings. Research the history of these labels, as well as all the other labels that set R&B soul music into motion. There are many books, biographies, and videos that chronicle the path of R&B soul music and its regional differences. It would be futile to try to interpret these sounds without being familiar with the overall influence these record labels had on the music.

PRACTICE TIPS

As you practice these drills, critique your own playing – and keep note of your progress. Play with a metronome or sequencer click to gauge and improve your rhythmic acuity. A metronome is preferable to a drum machine or pattern; with a metronome, you will be responsible for keeping time as well as playing the part in time. Though it can be challenging, several weeks' hard work will improve your rhythm skills. As a general rule, use quarter-note clicks; however, half- or whole-note clicks can be used for playing ballads.

Additionally, play without a metronome, forcing yourself to keep a steady beat. Record yourself playing these parts without the click and see where and when you speed up or slow down. This will help achieve a good balance between playing in time and will enhance your ability to accompany singers and play with other musicians. In each example, a target tempo marking is provided. Start with a self-imposed slow tempo and gradually speed up until you have reached the desired tempo marking.

Learn each pattern by practicing each hand separately at first. Pay close attention to the key signatures, accidentals, voicings, and rhythms. Don't be in too much of a hurry, or you'll learn and reinforce mistakes. Be patient. Haste always causes errors, and it is unrewarding to correct something you should not have practiced in the first place. Keep in mind the five Ps of perfection: *Prior preparation prevents poor performance.*

If you want good results, it is vital to be consistent. Playing any style of music requires commitment. Don't expect to get better unless you make a time investment. Set aside at least an hour for your practice sessions. Practice is work, but it can be fun. If you set a goal and reach it, your practice has been productive, rewarding, and ultimately enjoyable. Take note of the four Ds of time management:

Drop it, delay it, delegate it, or *do it.* The ironic thing about this statement is that if you drop it, you can't really do it; if you delay it, it is still there waiting for you later; if you delegate it, someone else gets better while you don't. So you really don't have a choice! The fact is, you have to do the work.

Work on the weakest aspects of your playing. If you practice only what you already know, how can you improve those things you don't execute so well? Too often, keyboard players lack strong music-reading skills. If this is one of your weaknesses, get help from a teacher who reads music.

Most keyboard players need to practice their technique. We have provided several R&B soul etudes; however, there are more common exercises to utilize. These include routinely practicing scales, chords, and rhythms. There are many keyboard books that provide drills and examples of good, basic keyboard methodology. Select and study these texts, videos, and instructional methods. Choose an effective book you can grow with and learn from while working on the rudiments of R&B soul keyboards.

Practice each exercise in this book as if a teacher in a class assigned it. *Don't try to play all these examples in one day.* Work on only two or three at a time. If you make a mistake, isolate that particular part and play the transition over and over until you get it. You'll waste time and frustrate yourself if you start at the beginning of a drill only to stop at the same erroneous part each time you play it. If you are having problems with notes, rhythms, voicings, or coordination, isolate each beat within a drill, as necessary,

SOUL GROOVES

The following exercises are designed to emulate common R&B soul patterns. Repeat them continually until a groove is established.

Ex. 1: "Love Makes Women" (P)

Track 66

Ex. 2: "You Were Made to Love Me" (P)

Track 67

Ex. 3: "Think Better" (P)

Track 68

Ex. 4: "I Heard It Was a Grapefruit" (P)

Track 69

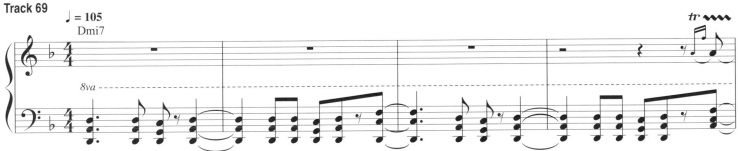

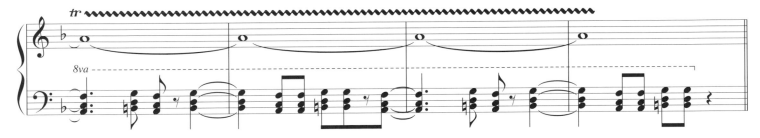

Ex 5: "Giving Up the Funk" (P)

Track 70

Ex. 6: "High Noon" (P)

Track 71

Ex. 7: "River Song" (P)

Track 72

Ex. 8: "The Postmark Song" (P)

Track 73

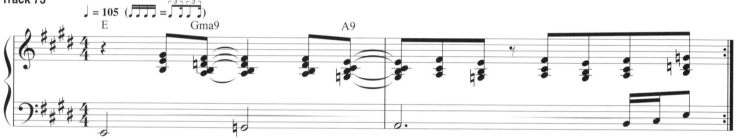

Ex. 9: "Yes I Am" (P)

Track 74

Ex. 10: "The Cattle Call Song" (P)

Track 75

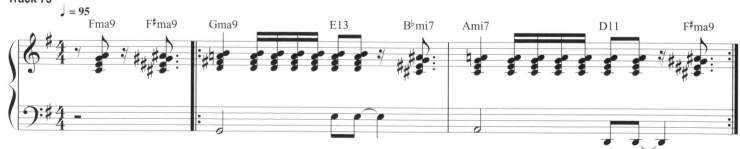

CHAPTER 8
SOUL BALLADS

The soul ballad is one of the most recognizable types of R&B soul song form, because the emotion and dynamics in its performance are easily identifiable. The soul ballad is normally played slowly, with emphasis on the vocal lines. The keyboard parts are usually chords with soft embellishments around the lead vocals. Singers like Aretha Franklin, Otis Redding, Marvin Gaye, Patti LaBelle, Ray Charles, and Gladys Knight are known for their emotional and explosive renditions of these songs.

The soul keyboard player often plays the intros of soul ballads with either electric or acoustic piano accompaniment. The beginning of The Jackson 5's "Who's Loving You?" is a good example, where the keyboard player plays a timeless riff for an intro. Another case in point is The Temptations' "I Can't Get Next to You." Many Motown ballads have piano introductions. Soul pianists routinely play slow arpeggios throughout the song. This allows other players in the rhythm section to play fills and rhythmic patterns. For instance, listen to Otis Redding's ballad "I've Been Loving You," in which the piano plays an intro with the correct tempo and establishes the key for the vocalist.

Time and again, R&B soul keyboard players employ string and piano parts in the intro and throughout various sections of the soul ballad. The string lines are usually melodic and dramatic. Additionally, pianists are required to play rhythmic chord patterns and even double-stop patterns within the song. As stated earlier, all the parts should be a musical representation of the song's lyrics; frequently, this means sounding repetitive chord patterns for a hypnotic effect. Shirley Brown's "Woman to Woman" starts with a soulful chord pattern while the guitarist plays echo-like effects for drama.

With songs like "I Miss You" by Harold Melvin & The Blue Notes, Philadelphia International records made the soul ballad popular during the 1970s. In this song, the keyboardist plays the chord pattern soulfully throughout. As the song moves further into the story, the pianist uses lots of double stops and blues licks, emphasizing the emotion of the singer. In Teddy Pendergrass's successful Philadelphia soul ballad "Love T.K.O.," the keyboard player cues up the electric piano sound to emote a melancholy mood and rich flavor that further emphasizes the lyrics and the singer's emotions.

KEEPING TEMPOS AND PLAYING WITH DYNAMICS

It is vitally important for the keyboard player to establish a steady beat and play with a good sense of dynamics. A song that has a solo piano intro can create a dilemma. The first question is, "How can I play the part in time to provide a definitive cue for the rest of the band?" The second question is, "How can I play a repeated or arpeggiated chord pattern with the right feel, rhythm, and groove?" The third question is, "Can I play the part with effective dynamics?" There are answers to all these questions; however, they could lead to either positive results or to negative results. One thing is certain: If you continue to play R&B soul keyboards, at some point you will encounter a situation where you will have to play an intro in time and cue the rest of the band into the song. Can you do it? It all depends on your preparation.

Many keyboard players have difficulty counting measures and playing at the same time. This problem lies with independence, not with counting. If you count downbeats along with subdivided beats, you should be better able to keep a regular pulse. Know the number of measures in the pattern, then place emphasis on the resolution chord or melody within the cadence. Tap your foot on the downbeats whenever you have to play a part in time by yourself.

To play the correct rhythm, feel, and groove for a soul ballad, listen to various recorded arrangements of the song. That way, you can hear how the keyboard player defined the parts of the song, as well as how they added soul to the ballad. I always imagine myself in the seat of the keyboard player who made the record. I ask myself what I would do under the same circumstances. Does it feel good to me? For example, what would I play on The Temptation's "I Wish It Would Rain"? Can I play the part? Do I have the right attitude? (Remember, attitude means a lot in this kind of music.) What kind of attitude am I bringing to this song? Do I have a broken heart, or am I asleep at the wheel?

Dynamics are also important to the song. Have you ever wondered why people tend to fall asleep while someone is talking to them or reciting a speech? This usually happens when there are no real highs or lows, or the story is unorganized and told without emphasis. What is the point? Literally, what is the point of your story? Musically, your keyboard part must have a point. By playing louder and softer in just the right sections of the ballad, we can convey this dynamic concept. We can also add *ritards* or *rallentandos* to our patterns whenever and wherever it is feasible.

SOUL BALLAD EXAMPLES

Ballad 1: I Am Your Man

To create the mood of this soulful example, the piano should have a gentle touch while still maintaining the tension generated by the L.H. pattern.

Ex. 1: "I Am Your Man" (P)

Track 76

Ballad 2: Ever Love a Woman?

In this example, the slightly aggressive, repetitive effect pushes the beat forward. Notice the blues-like inflections in this 3/4 pattern. Play it with a gospel flavor.

Ex. 2: "Ever Love a Woman?" (P)

Track 77

Ballad 3: Both of Us

Here, you want a lightly articulated sound, especially on the 16th notes. The repetitive effect adds to the mood of this soulful ballad.

Ex. 3: "Both of Us" (P)

Track 78

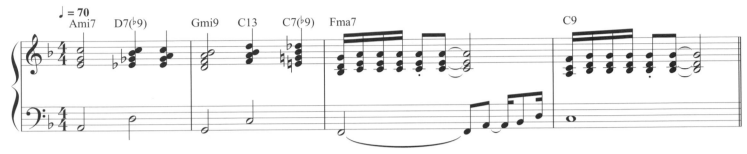

Ballad 4: Physical Feeling

Example 4 demonstrates a somewhat modern approach to floating a pad smoothly over a syncopated rhythm track.

Ex. 4: "Physical Feeling" (P)

Track 79

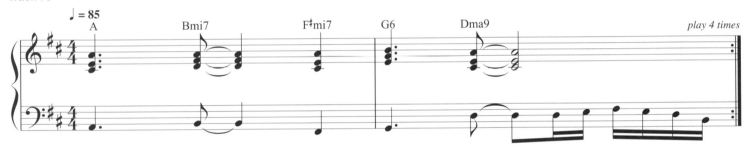

Ballad 5: Don't You Miss Me?

Note the many 1950s-style blues patterns in these four measures.

Ex. 5: "Don't You Miss Me?" (P)

Track 80

Ballad 6: Man to Woman

Here, a repetitive electric piano pattern creates drama and dynamics. Notice how the mood is set.

Ex. 6: "Man to Woman" (P)

Track 81

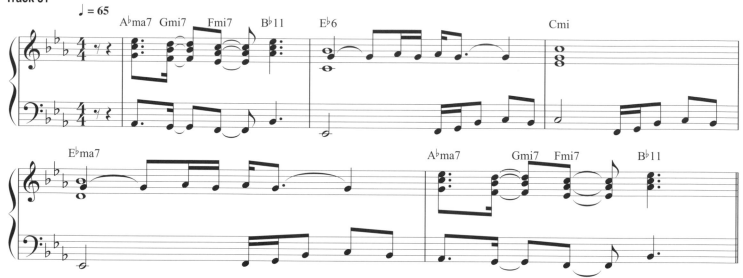

Ballad 7: Maybe I Love You

Try this combined variation of blues and gospel licks.

Ex. 7: "Maybe I Love You" (P)

Track 82

Ballad 8: You Knocked Me Out

Ex. 8: "You Knocked Me Out" (P)

Track 83

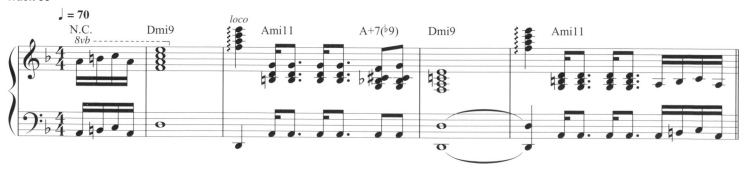

ACCOMPANYING A SINGER

To become a great R&B soul keyboard player, you must learn how to accompany a singer effectively. First ask yourself, "Who's in charge?" The answer is that you are in charge of the keyboard and the vocalist is in charge of the singing, but you should work together and interact with one another. As stated earlier, you need to be able to give solid cues to anyone you are playing with. In the case of a singer, this process becomes magnified.

Establish eye contact with the singer and make sure he/she is ready for you to begin the intro. Singers can get nervous and out of breath easily, so they often need feedback from their audience. When this is the case, you must be able to either improvise some related patterns or passages or play a refrain of the song until the singer is ready to start. This is common in the gospel church and in jazz, but not generally the case in R&B soul.

Many R&B soul vocalists like grandiose intros and piano parts. This could mean you have to play lots of arpeggios, scales, L.H. pedal points, or licks. The melody of the song, setting up the tempo, and performing with dynamics are the main things you should keep in mind. Listen carefully to gospel and jazz piano players to learn some of these techniques.

When you accompany a singer, your responsibility is greater. If you inadvertently make a mistake, don't compound the situation by belaboring it. If you play a wrong note or count incorrectly, let it go. You can't change the past. What you must do, however, is maintain the groove. If the error placed you a beat behind, catch up and maintain the rest of the song within the same beat. The only way to do this is with routine practice of recovery techniques. Here's a recipe for that:

1) Learn the song.

2) Practice the song three times straight and take note of problem spots, transitions, dynamics, tempo changes, etc.

3) Perform the song straight through, do or die.

4) Repeat the first three steps as many times as necessary.

5) Pack up your keyboard and play the gig.

Though there are many other points to be aware of, experience is the best teacher, especially when it comes to accompanying a singer. Watch live performances or videos of R&B soul keyboard players to get a handle on the intangibles of successful accompaniment.

CHAPTER 9

L.H. CHORDS WITH R.H. STRINGS

The modern R&B soul keyboard player often has to double a string line while holding down the chord progression. This can be difficult, no matter how simple each individual line may seem. In this chapter, we will examine several oft-used L.H./R.H. combinations of keyboard parts.

Although it is possible to play L.H. melodies and R.H. chords, it is far more common to play L.H. chords and R.H. melodies, since the keyboard's range from the middle register to its highest note is most conducive for melodies. This is also because so many people are naturally right-handed; the piano keyboard was designed primarily for right-handed dexterity. The left hand serves to perform more secondary musical chores.

R.H. priority voice leading

L.H. chord, R.H. melody

R&B soul keyboard players from the 1970s to the present have traditionally positioned electric pianos underneath a clavinet, organ, or synthesizer mounted atop the piano. When a keyboardist plays L.H. chord parts, his/her body must now be positioned slightly to the right of the center of the keyboard stack, considering the middle register of the electric piano below is where the L.H. chords are now to be played.

PLAYING MULTIPLE KEYBOARDS

When you play L.H. chords on a lower electric piano while playing R.H. melodies on another keyboard, a challenge occurs: You have to account for the new R.H. melodic range. It has shifted one octave because you have repositioned yourself. You could simply cross your right arm in front of your body, but this solution is somewhat awkward and may prevent you from reading music and obstruct your vision of the L.H. keyboard part. Transposing the range of the L.H. electric piano up one octave or the R.H. strings keyboard down one octave is another option to consider. This is probably the most viable answer; however, you must re-transpose the keyboards back to their original range after every two-handed performance. It may seem like too much to remember, but the 1970s R&B soul keyboard players had to play three or more keyboards with no modern transposition buttons, making all the necessary adjustments physically to coordinate parts.

Double keyboard set-up

Playing multiple keyboards can be challenging, but nowadays it is quite fascinating and necessary. It's a good idea to line up both keyboards so that their middle Cs are parallel with one another; that way, all the keys will be in vertical alignment with each other.

WHAT IF I HAVE ONLY ONE KEYBOARD?

Mulit-keyboard setup

You may be wondering how to play multiple parts on one keyboard. In the '70s, this would have been impossible, but now there are keyboards with split functions that allow you to sound a L.H. piano with a R.H. string part simultaneously. If you haven't already purchased a keyboard, this may be the type you are looking for.

Even if you don't currently own two keyboards, it will be to your advantage to have experience with multi-keyboards. There is a simple way to practice multiple keyboard lines on one keyboard: Use the middle register range for the L.H. and two octaves above that range for the R.H. melody. You won't necessarily have the string sound in thc R.H., but at least the part will be correct. This limitation will help you determine whether two keyboards are necessary for you. Remember: "Necessity is the mother of invention."

ATTACK, DECAY, SUSTAIN, RELEASE REVISITED

At this point in your study, you are aware that it is not advisablc to apply the same articulation of piano parts to string parts, for example. This is magnified when you have to play different articulations in each hand simultaneously, so be careful with attacks, sustaining notes, decaying notes, and release points. Be equally cautious when there is a disparity in L.H. and R.H. dynamics.

L.H. CHORDS WITH R.H. STRINGS EXAMPLES

If you are still having trouble coordinating both hands, continue practicing the etudes presented in Chapter 4. The following examples feature piano or organ chords in the L.H. and string parts in the R.H. They contain rhythmic syncopation distributed between both hands. They are two-hand keyboard patterns similar to those found in common R&B soul songs.

Ex. 1: "Lying Faces" (P)
Track 84

Ex. 2: "The Fool" (P)

Track 85

 Ex. 3: "It's Going Around" (P)

Track 86

 Ex. 4: "In the Neighborhood" (P)

Track 87

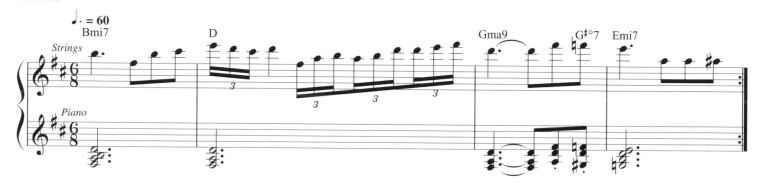

 Ex. 5: "W.S. Still Happening" (P)

Track 88

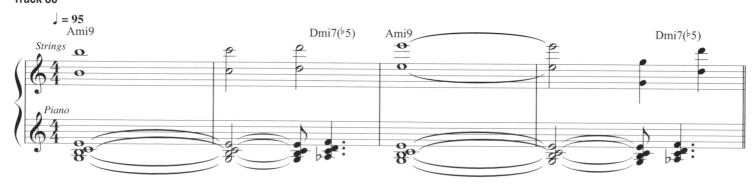

Ex. 6: "Only I Can Love You" (P)

Track 89

 Fig. 7: "Who Are You?" (P)

Track 90

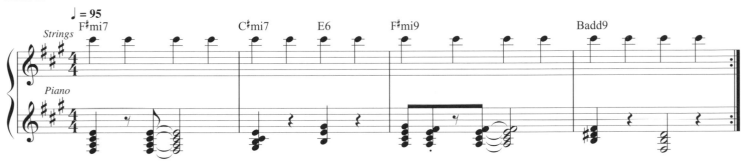

 Ex. 8: "Keep On Playing" (P)

Track 91

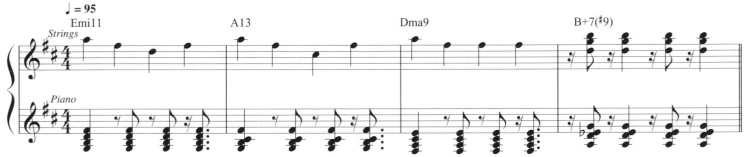

CHAPTER 10
L.H. CHORDS WITH R.H. HORNS

The modern R&B soul keyboardist often has to double brass or woodwind lines while holding down the chord progression. Performing L.H. piano or organ parts on one keyboard and R.H. horn parts on another is the most common way of doing this. In this chapter, we will continue the two-hand independence drills explored in the last chapter. We will also learn how L.H. melodic horn parts can be played while simultaneously executing R.H. piano-chord rhythms.

It should now be clearly understood that horns are articulated quite differently than piano or strings. You need to be able to make the technical adjustments required to play more realistic horn parts. If you are still having trouble with articulations or coordination, review Chapters 4 and 5.

UNDERSTANDING R&B SOUL HORN SECTIONS

The typical R&B soul horn section offers a unique blend: two trumpets, one alto sax, one tenor sax, and either one baritone sax or one trombone. A smaller conventional horn section consists of a trumpet, an alto sax, and a tenor sax. An R&B soul arrangement regularly contains more unison lines than harmony. The harmony normally occurs during bridge sections or refrains.

R&B horn arrangements frequently have dynamic trumpet and baritone sax range disparities, hits, fall-offs, swells, trills, and bent notes. Soul horn arrangements usually have lush harmonies, smooth legato melodic lines, muted trumpet or flügelhorn, soprano sax, and flute instrumentation. Since a keyboard will attempt to emulate these sounds and approaches to R&B soul music, study horn arrangements and listen carefully to how notes are typically played by each wind instrument. This will provide valuable insight into how to think like a horn player.

When you play L.H. chords and R.H. horn parts, the horn part can occasionally sound too thin. This happens because, time and again, trumpet and sax lines are doubled by a lower horn such as trombone or baritone sax. Since your L.H. will be playing a piano or organ chord, the most depth you can get from your R.H. is octave unison lines. You can solve this problem by using the layer function on your multi-timbral keyboard, stacking sounds like trumpet, alto sax, and trombone simultaneously. If you do not have a multi-timbral keyboard, try using the EQ controls on your amplifier to add more lows to your horn parts.

It is difficult to articulate some of the previously mentioned horn characteristics, such as swells, fall-offs, and glisses. Try simulating this with a sample played by a sampling keyboard. This is effective when combined with a synthesized horn sound. It is possible to MIDI the two sounds together for greater musical authenticity. In most cases, you must rely on your finger articulation and keyboard touch to make it sound real. This can often be considerably challenging, though it is not impossible.

Remember that horn players cannot play indefinitely, so take periodic breaks, methodically choosing your rest points. Do not play parts a horn section would not play. It's a good thing trumpet players can't play high notes all the time. It would be unbearable to listen to that screeching frequency all night long. (If only someone would tell the poor keyboard player not to play the high trumpet sound on his synthesizer all night!) Study horn arrangements in order to think like a horn player.

R&B SOUL HORN PARTS CHARACTERISTICS

Horn parts from the R&B soul songs of the 1950s contained many cliché lines and motifs. These familiar patterns included the use of trilled-third intervals, dominant-chord blasts, minor-second melodies played by the baritone sax, chromatic half-step ninth-chord bent notes, staccato eighth-note rhythms, and unison swells.

L.H. CHORD WITH R.H. HORN EXAMPLES

The following examples contain rhythmic syncopation between the hands. These exercises are similar to horn parts regularly found in R&B soul songs. Be aware of the dynamic blend necessary when playing L.H. piano or organ parts simultaneously with R.H. horn parts.

Track 92

Ex. 1: "Love's Still There" (P)

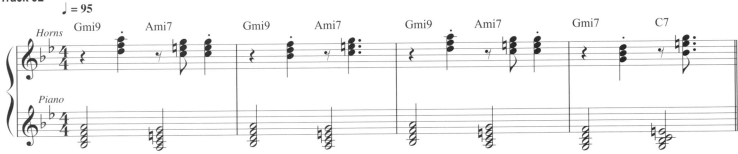

Track 93

Ex. 2: "In a Minute" (P)

This example calls for an organ sound for the L.H. chord groove. Be sure to use some of the organ characteristics presented in chapter 3 (*gliss*, etc.).

Track 94

Fig. 7: "Ex. 3: "Sooky, Sooky Na" (P)

A clavinet sound is employed for the L.H. chord groove. Even though the clavinet is normally played staccato, you should articulate a light touch while maintaining rhythmic accuracy.

Ex. 4: "You're So Generous" (P)

Track 95

In the following example, the L.H. sounds the horn melody while the R.H. simultaneously plays the eighth-note triplet piano part. The piano is played in the R.H. because of the octave range of the eighth-note triplets. You might need to transpose the range of your keyboard to play the horn part in the appropriate register.

Ex. 5: "Summer Daze" (P)

Track 96

Ex. 6: "Make a Better Way" (P)

Track 97

Track 98

Ex. 7: "I Got a Good Woman" (P)

Track 99

Ex. 8: "I Can't Tell You Nuthin'" (P)

RESOURCE MATERIALS

Throughout this book, I have encouraged you to read more and watch informative videos on R&B soul music. Aside from the thousands of recordings currently on the market, there could also be an unlimited supply of R&B soul music at your disposal. I am referring to your local radio station, which may be playing R&B soul oldies. Many of those classic R&B soul artists have box CD sets available and sometimes the record companies reissue old songs.

Some of the books and autobiographies I recommend that you read are:
The Death of R&B, Funk, Black Music, Billboard's Top Number One Hits, Berry Gordy's *To Be Loved, Marvin Gaye,* Diana Ross's *Call Her Miss Ross,* Michael Jackson's *Moonwalker, James Brown, Aretha Franklin, Sly & The Family Stone,* Hal Leonard R&B songbooks, *The Big Book of Rhythm & Blues,* and *The Motown Album.*

Some of the videos I recommend that you watch are:
B.B. King *King of the Blues, Bluesland, PBS History of Rock & Roll Collection, Albert King,* Stevie Wonder *Songs in the Key of Life, Frankie Beverly & Maze, Earth, Wind & Fire, Kool & The Gang,* The Jackson's *The American Dream,* Michael Jackson's *Moonwalker, Prince, Parliament/Funkadelic, Bootsy's Rubber Band, Maceo, Fred & Pee Wee, The Show,* VH1—*Seven Days Of Soul, Curtis Mayfield, Superfly, Marvin Gaye, Motown 25 and 40, History of Soul Music, Luther Vandross, Teddy Pendergrass, Gladys Knight, Ray Charles,* Tina Turner's *What's Love Got to Do with It, Wattstax,* Sinbad's *Summer Soul Festival Vol. 1–4, Soul to Soul, When We Were Kings,* and *The Blues Brothers.*

RECOMMENDED ARTISTS

I highly recommend that you listen to all the following artists:
The Platters; Bessie Smith; The Moonglows; The Ink Spots; The Coasters; The Drifters; The Dells; The Flamingos; Count Basie; Duke Ellington; Louis Jordan; Louis Armstrong; Earl Father Hines; Eubie Blake; Fats Domino; Bo Diddley; Nat King Cole; B.B. King; James Brown; Chuck Berry; Sam Cooke; Muddy Waters; Ray Charles; Freddie King; T-Bone Walker; Jackie Wilson; Albert King; Aretha Franklin; Brook Benton; Otis Redding; Joe Tex; Booker T & The MGs; Clarence Carter; Ben E. King; Jerry Butler; The Chi-Lites; Curtis Mayfield; The Impressions; The Contours; Jr. Walker & The Allstars; Jimmy Castor; The Delfonics; The Intruders; Blue Magic; The Persuasions; The Moments; Etta James; Isley Brothers; The Jackson 5; Gladys Knight; Motown; Lou Rawls; Sam & Dave; Sly & The Family Stone; The Spinners; Johnny Taylor; The Stylistics; Rufus Thomas; Ike & Tina Turner; Johnny Guitar Watson; Dionne Warwick; Stevie Wonder; Marvin Gaye; Chaka Kahn; Earth, Wind & Fire; Kool & The Gang; Chic; Heatwave; Philadelphia International; Barry White; Parliament; Ohio Players; The Whispers; The Dramatics; Prince; Jam & Lewis; Babyface; Teddie Riley; Luther Vandross; Oleta Adams; Whitney Houston; MeChell NdegeOchello; Erykah Badu; Incognito; Mariah Carey.

Additionally, check out these individual players:

Keyboard Player	Group/Artist	Recording
Otis Spann	Muddy Waters, etc.	Hoochie Coochie Man
Lafayette Leake	Koko Taylor, etc.	Wang Dang Doodle
Carl Banks	Etta James	Tell Mama
Dewey Oldham	Etta James, Chess, etc.	Your Precious Love
Leonard Caston	Chess session, Fontella B.	Rescue Me
Charles Brown	(himself)	Merry X-mas Baby
Ray Charles	blues sessions, etc.	What I Say?
Barry Beckett	Muscle Shoals, Aretha	Do Right Woman
Perry Kibble	Taste of Honey	Boogie Oogie Oogie
Billy Stewart	Chess	I Do Love You
Richard Tee	Aretha, Atlantic sessions	Just the 2 of Us
Thom Bell	Stylistics, Philly Writer	Stop, Look, Listen
Charles Stepney	Chess, Dells EWF prod.	Oh What a Night
Fats Domino	early R&B, blues sessions	Blueberry Hill
Professor Longhair	Orleans Blues sessions	
Ramsey Lewis	Chess sessions, early trio jazz	The In Crowd
Earl Van Dyke	Motown sessions	Heard It Through the Grapevine
Marvin Gaye	Motown sessions	Trouble Man
Freddie Perren	Motown sessions	Got to Be There
Joe Hunter	Motown sessions	Fingertips Pt. 2
Eddie Holland	Motown sessions	ABC
Stevie Wonder	Motown sessions	I Wish
D.J. Rogers	Columbia sessions	Say You Love Me
Latimore	(himself)	Let's Straighten It Out
Leon Huff	Philly sessions	If You Don't Know Me
Lenny Pakula	Philly sessions	When Will I See You?
Dexter Wansell	Philly sessions	Armed & Dangerous
Ron Kersey	Philly sessions	Back Stabbers
Donny Hathaway	Atlantic sessions	This Christmas
Allen Toussaint	Orleans, sessions	Lady Marmalade
Sly Stone Stewart	Sly & Family Stone	Wanna Take You Higher
Rose Stone Steward	Sly & Family Stone	Family Affair
Timmy Thomas	(himself)	Why Can't We Live
Leon Hayward	(himself), sessions	Bad Mamma Jamma
James Ingram	Quincy Jones, sessions	Bad Mamma Jamma
Leroy Flick Hodges	Al Green, W. Mitchell	Love & Happiness
Isaac Hayes	Stax sessions	Shaft
Skip Scarborough	Columbia sessions	Love Changes
Jerry Peters	Sony sessions	
Lonnie Jordan	War	Me & Baby Brother
Ricky West	Kool & the Gang	Hollywood Swinging
Ronnie Bell	Kool & the Gang	Summer Madness
Larry Dunn	Earth, Wind & Fire	Shining Star
George Duke	sessions, (himself)	Reach for It
Billy Beck	Ohio Players	Skintight
William Bryant	Marvin Gaye	Give It Up
Ronnie Foster	Stevie Wonder	Sunshine of My Life
Greg Phillingaines	Michael Jackson	Thriller
Victor Nix	Rolls Royce	Carwash
Michael Nash	Rolls Royce	I Wanna Get Next to You
Larry Ferguson	Hot Chocolate	You Sexy Thing
Angela Winbush	sessions, (herself)	Your Smile
Herbie Hancock	sessions, (himself)	Chameleon

Wayne Vaughan	Brothers Johnson	Blam
Robert Sam	Graham Central Station	The Jam
Herschell Happiness	Graham Central Station	The Jam
Billy Preston	Beatles, sessions, etc.	Out a Space
Chris Jasper	Isley Brothers	Live It Up
Patrice Rushen	sessions, (herself)	Remind Me
Booker T Jones	M.G.s, Stax, etc.	Hip Hug Her
Jimmy Davis	LTD	Love Ballad
Claude Cave Coffee	Mandrill	Fencewalk
Aretha Franklin	session, (herself)	Think
Valerie Simpson	Motown sessions	You're All I Need
Marvin Yancy	Stax sessions	Leaving Me
Chuck Jackson	Natalie Cole	This Will Be
Milan Williams	Commodores	Machine Gun
Chester Thompson	Tower of Power	What Is Hip?
Kevin Murphy	Rufus, Chaka Khan	Tell Me Something Good
Hawk Dave Wolinsky	Chaka Khan	Ain't Nobody
Nate Morgan	Rufus	Do You Love What You Feel
Harry Wayne Casey	KC & the Sunshine Band	That's the Way I Like It
Michael Ibo Cooper	Third World	Try Jah Love
Lionel Ritchie	Commodores, (himself)	Easy
Mtume	Stephanie Mills, (session)	Juicy Fruit
Rod Temperton	Heatwave, Michael Jackson	Thriller
Bernie Worrell	Parliament, Bootsy, etc.	Flashlight
Mickey Atkins	Funkadelic	Standing on the Verge
Charlie Wilson	Gap Band	Shake
Kashif	BT Express, Whitney, etc.	Do It till Satisfied
Matt Fink Doctor	Prince	1999
Lisa Coleman	Prince, Wendi & Lisa	Let's Go Crazy
Phillip Woo	Maze	Joy & Pain
Sam Porter	Maze	Feel That You're Feelin'
Jimmy McGriff	session, (himself)	I Got a Woman
Calvin Duke	Heatwave	Boogie Nights
Keith Harrison	Heatwave	Groove Line
Jimmy Jam	The Time, sessions	Nasty Boys
Monte Moore	The Time	777-9311
Greg Johnson	Cameo	Knights by Night
Thomas Campbell	Cameo	Single Life
Hubert Eaves	20th Century sessions	If I Were Your Woman
Harry Whitaker	20th Century sessions	Sweetness Is Weakness
Babyface	Solar sessions, etc.	I'm Your Baby Tonight
Leon Sylvers	Solar sessions, Whispers	Rock Steady
Gary Wilkins	Solar sessions, Lakeside	Raid
Norman Beavers	Solar sessions, Shalamar	Second Time Around
Nat Adderly, Jr.	Luther Vandross, sessions	Never Too Much
Felton Pilate	Con Funk Shun	Love's Train
Danny Thomas	Con Funk Shun	F-Fun
Delbert Taylor	Slave	Slide
Charles & Sam Carter	Slave	Just a Touch of Love
Charles Bradley	Slave	Snap Out You
Attala Zane Giles	EWF, Mothers Finest	Legs & Lipstick
Walter "Junie" Morrison	P-Funk, Ohio Players	Ecstasy
Chucki Booker	sessions, himself	Turned Away
DeAngelo	sessions, himself	You're My Lady

FOUR DECADES OF FUNK

1960s

Gospel
James Cleveland
Mahalia Jackson
The Soul Stirrers

R&B
Ray Charles
James Brown
Wilson Pickett
Booker T & the MGs
Isley Brothers
Atlantic Artists
Stax Artists

Blues/Rock
Muddy Waters
Howlin' Wolf
Chuck Berry
Little Richard
Bo Diddley
B.B. King

Jazz & Jazz-Rock
Miles Davis Quintet
Herbie Hancock
John Coltrane
Jazz Crusaders
Sun Ra
Ramsey Lewis
Donald Byrd
Art Blakey
Horace Silver
Charles Mingus

Soul
James Brown
Aretha Franklin
Motown Artists
Impressions
Otis Redding
Parliaments
Isaac Hayes

Black Rock
Jimi Hendrix
Sly and the Family Stone
Bar-Kays
Meters

1970s

Soulful Funk
Stevie Wonder
Curtis Mayfield
Marvin Gaye
Temptations
O'Jays
Barry White
Earth, Wind & Fire
Commodores
Rufus and Chaka Khan
Heatwave
Con Funk Shun
Rose Royce
Maze

Mega Funk
JBs/James Brown
Parliament
Funkadelic
Kool & the Gang
Bootsy's Rubber Band
Isley Brothers
Rufus
War
Graham Central Station
Average White Band
Mandrill
Tower of Power
Commodores
Ohio Players
Slave
Brick
Cameo
Undisputed Truth

Jazz-Funk
Roy Ayers
Donald Byrd
Stanley Clarke
Crusaders
Miles Davis
George Duke
Funk Inc.
Herbie Hancock
Ramsey Lewis
Grover Washington, Jr.

Early Go Go/House
B.T. Express
Brass Construction
Chic
Fatback
K.C. & the Sunshine Band

1980s

Raw Funk
Cameo
Dazz Band
Gap Band
Rick Jame
Klymaxx
Lakeside
One Way
Prince
Slave

'80s Funk Pop
Janet Jackson
Michael Jackson
Chaka Khan
Kool & the Gang
Maze
Midnight Star
S.O.S. Band
Full Force
Whispers
Ready for the World

African Acid
Africa Bambaataa
George Clinton
Defunkt
Fishbone
Herbie Hancock
Living Colour
Tackhead
Trouble Funk/Go Go

1990s

Contemporary R&B
Bobby Brown
Guy
Chucki Booker
Lauryn Hill
Dru Hill
Mint Condition
Brand New Heavies

Hip Hop
A Tribe Called Quest
Arrested Development
De La Soul
Digable Planets
Digital Underground
Fugees
Busta Rhymes

Gangsta Rap
Dr. Dre
Eazy E
Ice Cube
Ice-T
N.W.A.
Snoop Doggy Dogg
Too Short
Tupac

Political Rap
Kam
KRS One/BDP
Paris
Public Enemy
X-Clan

Funk Rock
MeChell NdegeOchello
New Rubber Band
O.G. Funk
Red Hot Chili Peppers

ACKNOWLEDGMENTS

I would like to dedicate this book to my loving and extraordinary wife Cheryl Wade Brewer, my beautiful and talented daughter Angel M. Wade Brewer, and my wonderful mother Deborah O. Brewer, all of whom have given me encouragement and inspiration.

There are many people who have provided encouragement and have played an important role in my development as a man, musician, and educator. I would like to thank Stan Coleman, Reggie Dellard, Arvell Keithley, Brian Simms, Dave Smith, Larry Davis, Sidney Woods, Emory Washington, Charles Hughes, William Vincent, Mindy Nathanson, Kenny Rogers, Pernell Garner, Mary Etta Boyd, Willard Pugh, Sekou Olatunji, Robert Helmer, Jim Collier, Dr. Eloise Jarvis and the staff of the Webster University Music Department, and Jerry Kovarsky Korg.

Thanks to everyone at Hal Leonard Corporation.

Very special thanks to: Dean Brown, Dino Monoxoles, Meri Ka Ra, Erica Byrd, Keith Wyatt, and all of the staff at Musicians Institute.

I would like to thank the following musicians whom I have had the honor of working with and learning from: Freddie White, Verdine White, Larry Dunn, Lui Lui Satterfield, Phenix Horns, Ralph Johnson, B.B. King, Wanda Vaughn & The Emotions, Shirley Brewer, Tom Brechtlein, Roscoe Beck, Bernard Purdie, Novi Novog, Lee Sklar, Rocco Prestia, Marlo Henderson, Derf Reklaw Raheem, Munyungo, Ed Rowe, Patrice Rushen, Thomas Dolby, Cat Gray, Carl Schroeder, Tim Bogert, Fred Dinkins, James Woods, Norman Brown, Scott Henderson, Kongo, Robben Ford, Athoas Brown, Roscoe Lee Brown, and Stevie Wonder.

I would like to pay tribute to four musicians I have had the pleasure of working with who are no longer with us: Marlon Travis, Terry Jackson, Don Myrick, and Donnell Wade. May your memory linger on like the beautiful music you made!

Lastly I would like to thank the following people for all their musical and technical expertise that went into the making of this book: Ermias Mesghenna, Gail Johnson, Sekou Olatunji, Shane Weedman, Hyun Cho, Doo Lee, Kostas K, Tracee Lewis, Ken Williams, Chris Torrey, Jeanette Mishler, and Isis Nefertari Nubian.

–Henry Soleh Brewer

ABOUT THE AUTHOR

Henry Soleh Brewer, also known as Sol-Eh-Areh, has been a professional musician for nearly four decades. He started his career with a St. Louis-area band called Constellation, then went on to play with such greats as B.B. King, The O'Jays, The Emotions, and members of Earth, Wind & Fire. Henry is also a songwriter/producer with his own recording studio. He has recorded keyboards on Coors beer radio jingles, *Home Improvement* television commercials, and the films *Police Academy 2, Bob Roberts, Nemesis,* and *Fast Getaway 2,* among others.

Henry was a founding instructor in the Keyboard Technology program at Musicans Institute in Hollywood, California. He has written several books and has performed on a number of instructional CDs and videos, including his own blues keyboards instructional video. Henry continues to teach blues, R&B, soul, and groove styles at Musicians Institute.

KEYBOARD STYLE SERIES

THE COMPLETE GUIDE!

These book/audio packs provide focused lessons that contain valuable how-to insight, essential playing tips, and beneficial information for all players. From comping to soloing, comprehensive treatment is given to each subject. The companion audio features many of the examples in the book performed either solo or with a full band.

BEBOP JAZZ PIANO
by John Valerio

This book provides detailed information for bebop and jazz keyboardists on: chords and voicings, harmony and chord progressions, scales and tonality, common melodic figures and patterns, comping, characteristic tunes, the styles of Bud Powell and Thelonious Monk, and more.

00290535 Book/CD Pack..$18.99

BEGINNING ROCK KEYBOARD
by Mark Harrison

This comprehensive book/CD package will teach you the basic skills needed to play beginning rock keyboard. From comping to soloing, you'll learn the theory, the tools, and the techniques used by the pros. The accompanying CD demonstrates most of the music examples in the book.

00311922 Book/CD Pack..$14.99

BLUES PIANO
by Mark Harrison

With this book/audio pack, you'll learn the theory, the tools, and even the tricks that the pros use to play the blues. Covers: scales and chords; left-hand patterns; walking bass; endings and turnarounds; right-hand techniques; how to solo with blues scales; crossover licks; and more.

00311007 Book/Online Audio $19.99

BOOGIE-WOOGIE PIANO
by Todd Lowry

From learning the basic chord progressions to inventing your own melodic riffs, you'll learn the theory, tools and techniques used by the genre's best practicioners.

00117067 Book/Online Audio $17.99

BRAZILIAN PIANO
by Robert Willey and Alfredo Cardim

Brazilian Piano teaches elements of some of the most appealing Brazilian musical styles: choro, samba, and bossa nova. It starts with rhythmic training to develop the fundamental groove of Brazilian music.

00311469 Book/Online Audio $19.99

CONTEMPORARY JAZZ PIANO
by Mark Harrison

From comping to soloing, you'll learn the theory, the tools, and the techniques used by the pros. The full band tracks on the CD feature the rhythm section on the left channel and the piano on the right channel, so that you can play along with the band.

00311848 Book/CD Pack..$17.99

COUNTRY PIANO
by Mark Harrison

Learn the theory, the tools, and the tricks used by the pros to get that authentic country sound. This book/audio pack covers: scales and chords, walkup and walkdown patterns, comping in traditional and modern country, Nashville "fretted piano" techniques and more.

00311052 Book/Online Audio $19.99

GOSPEL PIANO
by Kurt Cowling

Discover the tools you need to play in a variety of authentic gospel styles, through a study of rhythmic devices, grooves, melodic and harmonic techniques, and formal design. The accompanying audio features over 90 tracks, including piano examples as well as the full gospel band.

00311327 Book/Online Adio $17.99

INTRO TO JAZZ PIANO
by Mark Harrison

From comping to soloing, you'll learn the theory, the tools, and the techniques used by the pros. The accompanying audio demonstrates most of the music examples in the book. The full band tracks feature the rhythm section on the left channel and the piano on the right channel, so that you can play along with the band.

00312088 Book/Online Audio $19.99

JAZZ-BLUES PIANO
by Mark Harrison

This comprehensive book will teach you the basic skills needed to play jazz-blues piano. Topics covered include: scales and chords • harmony and voicings • progressions and comping • melodies and soloing • characteristic stylings.

00311243 Book/Online Audio $17.99

JAZZ-ROCK KEYBOARD
by T. Lavitz

Learn what goes into mixing the power and drive of rock music with the artistic elements of jazz improvisation in this comprehensive book and CD package. This instructional tool delves into scales and modes, and how they can be used with various chord progressions to develop the best in soloing chops.

00290536 Book/CD Pack..$17.95

LATIN JAZZ PIANO
by John Valerio

This book is divided into three sections. The first covers Afro-Cuban (Afro-Caribbean) jazz, the second section deals with Brazilian influenced jazz – Bossa Nova and Samba, and the third contains lead sheets of the tunes and instructions for the play-along CD.

00311345 Book/CD Pack..$17.99

MODERN POP KEYBOARD
by Mark Harrison

From chordal comping to arpeggios and ostinatos, from grand piano to synth pads, you'll learn the theory, the tools, and the techniques used by the pros. The online audio demonstrates most of the music examples in the book.

00146596 Book/Online Audio $17.99

NEW AGE PIANO
by Todd Lowry

From melodic development to chord progressions to left-hand accompaniment patterns, you'll learn the theory, the tools and the techniques used by the pros. The accompanying 96-track CD demonstrates most of the music examples in the book.

00117322 Book/CD Pack..$16.99

POST-BOP JAZZ PIANO
by John Valerio

This book/audio pack will teach you the basic skills needed to play post-bop jazz piano. Learn the theory, the tools, and the tricks used by the pros to play in the style of Bill Evans, Thelonious Monk, Herbie Hancock, McCoy Tyner, Chick Corea and others. Topics covered include: chord voicings, scales and tonality, modality, and more.

00311005 Book/Online Audio $17.99

PROGRESSIVE ROCK KEYBOARD
by Dan Maske

You'll learn how soloing techniques, form, rhythmic and metrical devices, harmony, and counterpoint all come together to make this style of rock the unique and exciting genre it is.

00311307 Book/CD Pack..$19.99

R&B KEYBOARD
by Mark Harrison

From soul to funk to disco to pop, you'll learn the theory, the tools, and the tricks used by the pros with this book/audio pack. Topics covered include: scales and chords, harmony and voicings, progressions and comping, rhythmic concepts, characteristic stylings, the development of R&B, and more! Includes seven songs.

00310881 Book/Online Audio $19.99

ROCK KEYBOARD
by Scott Miller

Learn to comp or solo in any of your favorite rock styles. Listen to the audio to hear your parts fit in with the total groove of the band. Includes 99 tracks! Covers: classic rock, pop/rock, blues rock, Southern rock, hard rock, progressive rock, alternative rock and heavy metal.

00310823 Book/Online Audio $17.99

ROCK 'N' ROLL PIANO
by Andy Vinter

Take your place alongside Fats Domino, Jerry Lee Lewis, Little Richard, and other legendary players of the '50s and '60s! This book/audio pack covers: left-hand patterns; basic rock 'n' roll progressions; right-hand techniques; straight eighths vs. swing eighths; glisses, crushed notes, rolls, note clusters and more. Includes six complete tunes.

00310912 Book/Online Audio $18.99

SALSA PIANO
by Hector Martignon

From traditional Cuban music to the more modern Puerto Rican and New York styles, you'll learn the all-important rhythmic patterns of salsa and how to apply them to the piano. The book provides historical, geographical and cultural background info, and the 50+-tracks includes piano examples and a full salsa band percussion section.

00311049 Book/Online Audio $19.99

SMOOTH JAZZ PIANO
by Mark Harrison

Learn the skills you need to play smooth jazz piano – the theory, the tools, and the tricks used by the pros. Topics covered include: scales and chords; harmony and voicings; progressions and comping; rhythmic concepts; melodies and soloing; characteristic stylings; discussions on jazz evolution.

00311095 Book/Online Audio $17.99

STRIDE & SWING PIANO
by John Valerio

Learn the styles of the stride and swing piano masters, such as Scott Joplin, Jimmy Yancey, Pete Johnson, Jelly Roll Morton, James P. Johnson, Fats Waller, Teddy Wilson, and Art Tatum. This book/audio pack covers classic ragtime, early blues and boogie woogie, New Orleans jazz and more. Includes 14 songs.

00310882 Book/Online Audio $19.99

HAL•LEONARD®

www.halleonard.com